THE BEATLES
SENT TO COVENTRY

Pete Chambers

Cover photograph
The Beatles listen to Dora Bryan's "All I Want For Christmas is a Beatle"
on the radio in Coventry
Courtesy of Mirror Syndication International

Introducing This Book

I love many types of music; I can easily talk about say Bhangra music then onto Ska and rap, calling at classical, music hall and heavy rock on the way. If it's good music then it's good music, what more can I say! Well quite a lot really, I am always ready to talk music, especially those pioneers like Hank Williams and Hank Snow, Jimmie Rodgers, Leadbelly and Woody Guthrie. The men who would make a difference to what we would all know and love as rock n roll. It is all so obvious where this was all going with the power of hindsight. These would in turn have a profound effect on the next young musical upstarts waiting in the wings like Elvis, Buddy Holly, Jerry Lee Lewis, Chuck Berry and Little Richard. So the influence goes on to bands like The Rolling Stones and The Beatles. The Beatles inspiration to musicians and non-musicians alike would of course help to settle-down a relatively young music revolution we would know as pop music. Experimenting and defining the genre to such an extent that there are many books written on the subject of simply what the Fab Four did for music.

The Author on the repro bench 2005

Of course anyone who reads this book is all too aware of what those four lads from Liverpool did for popular culture. The thing with the Beatles is it always seemed so personal, becoming what did the Beatles do for me or for you?

So please allow me to be a little self-indulgent. will take you back to my memories, right back to the days of Please, Please Me. That may not sound too far back, but considering I was only eight at the time, then it's a proud achievement for someone who was quintessentially a child of the 70's, not the 60's. I was of course well aware of what was happening, my sister Sue was five years older than me and I'm grateful to her for being a pop fan of the sixties. It was because of her I soaked up all these sounds, though she would quickly grow out of the Beatles and move onto The Small Faces, The Troggs and the Walker Brothers.

Anyway back to Please, Please Me, my sister had borrowed the new LP from a friend, I can remember my Dad setting up my sister's EMI portable record player on the flower stand in the corner of the room (where we put the tree at Christmas). As to be expected Sis and me loved the new fab waxing, and so to a degree my Dad. My Mum would always be one of those people who were proud not to like the Beatles, so it was a miss for Mum. That kind of suited me at the time though (who wants your mum to dig your taste in music anyway?) Then there was my full name (Peter John George Chambers) that would invariably invoke a comment, like, "Were your parents Beatles fans?" Still does today, imagine if Peter Best had stayed on the drums! No I wasn't named after the Moptops by the way, John was my dad, George my Granddad and Pete was just a name they happened to like..

I recently found a sketchbook I had when I was coming up to the age of seven. In it I have drawn banks of amplifiers and a stage full of microphones and leads. proving that even then I was obsessed with music. Not that it needs much proving, there is a picture of me somewhere sat astride a toy dog with a ukulele in my hand. The instrument had two volume knobs stuck on it (the remains of the aforementioned record player), and some wool stuck to it's base to resemble the guitar lead. Yes it had to look the business. even my old cowboy waistcoat was turned inside out, and my sister wrote on it Pete and The Dragons, or something similar. The family would often get me to make a fool of myself, I couldn't play the uke' of course (lack of ability and strings), but I would pretend to be a Beatle, or Gerry Marsden. They were much the same of course, only when I did Gerry I was sussed enough to put my instrument right under my chin.

I don't remember too many Beatles memories for the next few years apart from seeing the Lady Madonna promo film on Top Of The Pops. It was not until around the time of The Beatles Double White Album that I became a big fan. I recall asking for that album for a Christmas present. My Mum & Dad ordered it from the catalogue, then made the mistake of hiding it in their wardrobe, so every time they left the house I would sneak a peak of it. I never played it but I adored the poster and those great colour portraits of the guys that came with it. It was actually a numbered mono copy, but I foolishly sold it to buy fags during my teenage nicotine addiction. I recall swapping stuff for "The Beatles Oldies but Goldies" LP, and going straight into the city from school to buy Abbey Road as soon as it was released. To my shame when I first heard about it I was convinced it was called Happy Road!

I would spend all my paper round money on Beatles singles and albums. In fact, that paper round prevented me from seeing a re-showing of The Magical Mystery Tour TV film. It coincided with my evening delivery and there were no video recorders in those days, I was not a happy boy. One scam I do remember pulling was claiming a kid at school was leaving for Australia and selling off his record collection. I persuaded my Mum to let me draw the money out of the bank to buy his copy of Let It Be (the boxed version, complete with book).

I got the money and was straight down to Jill Hanson's Record shop to buy a brand new copy of the just released album. I never did tell my Mum, God Bless Her. I ended up cutting up the box outer sleeve and taking pages out of the book to pin on my wall. It gives me no satisfaction to tell you this, as you will know that the Let It Be boxed version is worth well over £200 these days.

One fierce recollection is hearing at work that John Lennon had been shot. It was just so ludicrous I pretty much ignored it. I mean, why would anyone want to kill John, a man of peace, especially when the world was full of politicians who virtually courted assassination. I remember coming home, sitting with my food-tray on my knees, watching the news. There it was, the truth, John was dead and it was making no sense. It still doesn't. I sat there crying, not something I had done for many years. My Dad bless his soul looked at me not knowing what was going on. He said to me, "Why are you crying? He was only a pop star". But of course he wasn't just a pop star, he was part of my life, I grew up with him. OK, I never met John or any of the Beatles, but they were always there. The soundtrack to my life, and now some nobody psychopath had come and claimed a piece of Lennon history which he had no right to; and should have remained the twisted nobody he was and will always be. Since that day in December I have never spoken that man's name, and I never will, he doesn't deserve one for what he did.

In fact it even took me about ten years before I could ever play "Happiness Is A Warm Gun" again, such was the shock of it all. I had never been affected like this before. In fact it was probably the first death that ever hit me to such a great degree. The days that followed were filled with the usual 'sick' jokes; I just ignored them as much as possible. I guess we all did. Even as I write Yoko admits that after all these years she and Sean still find it hard to come to terms with. Worst of all is the thought of all those musical masterpieces we will now never hear. I visited New York a few years ago, I went to Strawberry Fields and reluctantly stood for a photo outside of the Dakota Building, I felt a sense of betrayal to John's memory, but I also felt that by having the picture taken would be an opportunity to move on. Despite being a musical journalist I'm still a fan, and I have done all the 'fan things', like the Abbey Road zebra crossing shot, The Magical History Tour in Liverpool. I went down to Abbey Road when George died, just to leave something on the wall that read "Within You Now Without You", the best I could think of at the time.

So although I have a love for thousands of records from hundreds of bands, the Mop Top legacy is never far away. As it is with my speciality subject that is local music (local as in Coventry & Warwickshire). My first book, Godiva Rocks (basically a musical encyclopaedia of local Coventry & Warwickshire music) included many Beatles facts, as have some of my subsequent Coventry Evening Telegraph columns entitled Backbeat (yes even that has Beatle connections).

Meeting Yoko in October 2005 was a thrill, and brought things into perspective for me as a Beatles fan. It also put the germ of the idea of this book into my mind. I was wary at first; I'm a Beatles fan as I mentioned, but not a Beatles expert by any means. I would hate to insult all of those people who know far more about the Fab Four than me. As I said, my specialist subject is Coventry and Warwickshire music, but when a band or artist moves into my jurisdiction then they become part of my subject, then I can claim them for myself. So I decided right or wrong that there was enough information to merit a book. It had a few things going for it. (1) It includes the most information I have seen about John and Yoko's visits to the city. (2) It puts to rest the myth of that Nuneaton concert and (3) it includes many rare and often unseen pictures of the boys, courtesy of The Coventry Evening Telegraph and Mirrorpix. Plus, it includes a lot of other pieces of trivia and information that may be of interest.

The first 36 pages of this book look at Beatles visits to the area in chronological order. From there we go into an A to Z of items that have two common connections-those are of course Coventry (and Warwickshire) and The Beatles (and the solo members of that band). Now read on…………..

The Co-op Hall, Nuneaton 5th October 1962

Some have claimed that this concert never took place; well sorry but this concert is not figment of a warped Beatle imagination but a reality, indeed it was also the day the Beatles released their first proper single, 'Love Me Do' (now there's a quiz question for you). The Beatles were second on the bill sandwiched between the headlining Buddy Brittain & the Regents and Rugby's Mighty Avengers in the support slot.

This would be the pre-fab four's first concert in this area (not The Matrix in Coventry, as has been stated). Dave 'Biffo' Beech drummer with the (Mighty) Avengers, remembers the gig clearly. "I recall they came out in brown suits and ties, with cream shirts. Even then you could tell there was something about them, despite the fact that only those up north knew anything about them. People just stopped and listened, they sounded good and fresh. It was also the day they had released their first single 'Love me Do', I can remember them saying that their new single is out today so go and buy it. After a great set they did just the one encore as I recall". I asked Dave if he got to speak to any of the guys? "Just the usual backstage banter, nothing in-depth, Ringo and George were pretty quiet whilst Lennon behaved like he was in charge, whereas you could sense it was Paul who was really driving the group". Tony Campbell, also of the Avengers, had his tale to tell of the night.

Above, The Co-op Hall Nuneaton, Left a very rare picture of Buddy Brittain, below left The Tribune advert for the show and below right The Avengers in Coventry. In 1963 They became the first Midlands beat outfit to play at the Cavern Club, they even have their name on the wall of fame.

CO-OPERATIVE BALLROOM, NUNEATON

TEEN BEAT
TONIGHT
BUDDY BRITTAIN
AND THE REGENTS

AND FOR THE FIRST TIME IN NUNEATON, THE FABULOUS NEW RECORDING GROUP

THE BEATLES
SUPPORTED BY THE AVENGERS

THE BIGGEST BEAT SHOW EVER!

7.45 to 11 pm. Admission: 5/-

"I remember the night at Nuneaton Co-op Hall very well, although I can't remember the date other than it was the Friday Love Me Do was released. Rockin' Reg Calvert was the promoter, and he had been running shows there for a long time as one of his regular do's. We worked there a lot as a support band, and he always booked a headliner with either one of his own bands and or other locals. The main group had arrived in a brown Bedford Dormobile type van parked outside, We walked in with our gear (up those ruddy stairs) to find a jam session going on with Ringo and Barney Peacock on drums, Lennon & Buddy Brittain on guitars with Pete Mist on Bass. George Harrison was upstairs in the dressing room playing his big acoustic Gibson. I asked Pete Mist later who the band was, and he said The Beatles. I said "Who", and Pete told me that they had worked with them at the Star Club Hamburg, and that they were the greatest rhythm and blues band he had seen. That was a compliment coming from Pete because he had been professional himself for a long time, and played in one of the best bands I knew at that time, Buddy Brittain & The Regents. They were one of the "house" bands run by Reg along with Danny Storm & the Strollers.

The Nuneaton audience had seen everything, and were generally not appreciative, usually more interested in fighting than watching. We regularly used to count the number of punters the bouncers threw down those (ruddy) stairs. The Beatles sent them wild with versions of What I'd Say, Money and other songs I had never heard before, including of course their new record. (not on Decca,- sorry Dick, ha-ha) You must remember that this was the era of the Shadows, and most of the groups were either adjusting their echo units or falling down tripping over guitar leads trying to do the Shadows Walk.

The Beatles were different, exciting, loud (no echo), and raw, with great voices & harmonies (5 hours a night in Germany does something to the voice) as well as looking good. They had dark colour suits I seem to remember, but it was before the "haircuts". I always remember standing with Pete in the wings and him pointing to John Lennon's toe curling up boots, as he rocked on, with a high-strung Rickenbacker. The big thing was how together they were. It showed that they had done many gigs and knew what each other was doing, or going to do. They were so professional and even then knew how to bow to an audience, very foreign to most of us. We learnt much later the value of rehearsal and presentation. My late father always said that the following morning I was raving about a silly named band that I would have put money on being big, I didn't realise just how big".

Sadly the promoter of that concert Reg Calvert was murdered in 1966, struck down by a shotgun over the rights to a pirate radio station. Though I did talk to his daughter Sue about that night. "Sadly, I didn't meet the Beatles" She explains, but my parents did. My father (Reg Calvert) sent various bands out to Germany to play in the same clubs as the Beatles

They were unknown and acted as a backing group to various singers that my parents managed and they made friends with the Beatles. When the Beatles returned from Germany my father had been told they were a good band, so he booked them into Nuneaton on that Friday night, and also another dance hall in Birmingham. That's why I didn't see them, as I always went to Nuneaton on the Saturday night to 'run' the dance".

Also in attendance that night was pop-mogul (to be) Pete Waterman, who reckoned there were around 700 people in the room that night, most of them going bananas. Summing up, check out the boys schedule and it shows they had a *lunchtime* gig at The Cavern on the 4th, thus giving them more time for the journey South! Then there's the advert for the show from the local Nuneaton Tribune newspaper. So more than enough proof that this gig did happen, game set and match to Nuneaton, no question, now get those Beatle books re-written!

The Beatles at The Matrix, 17th November 1962

The Matrix as it was. *Photograph courtesy of Mirror Syndication International*

This was The Beatles first time in Coventry, The Matrix basically a works canteen for Matrix Engineering. Although well out of town, it hosted some great talent in the 60's, bands like the Kinks, the Small Faces and The Rolling Stones all played here. It would continue hosting bands like Steppenwolf into the 70's when it finally closed.

The Beatles had returned from Hamburg on the 15th November. The event is documented in the motion picture "Let It Be" Between the songs "Dig It" and "Two of Us". Paul talks to a pretty uninterested John about George's worries of playing live again. Paul says to John, "When we came back from Hamburg and did Leicester De Montford Hall or wherever it was, Coventry! You know we played the ballroom and we had the worst first night thing, we were all nervous, it was terrible". Coventry was about the fourth time they had ventured so far south so this was a big gig for them. Though it's hard to think of the Beatles ever being nervous on stage, yet it was still an issue for them six years later during "Let It Be". The Ad for the concert proclaimed **Saturday November 17th-Scoop! Scoop! Scoop! Hit recorders of "Love Me Do", direct from their German tour The Beatles. The show was due to kick off at 7.45 and finish at 11.45,** with a licensed bar, buffet and even late buses. Tickets were available for 5/6 or 6/- and were available from Jill Hansons Record Shop 8 Market Way, Coventry and The Record Centre, Smithford Way, Coventry. The Beatles manager Brian Epstein was with them that night, (if you read below, he must have turned up later on his own) and told Coventry Standard scribe Andy Anderson that Please Please Me was to be the next single. One other guy who was there was John Harris, "A friend of mine" says John, "Tom Nicoll knew Ringo from the Rory Storm days and he told him that he was joining a new band called The Beatles and that he would be playing in Coventry. He said if we waited in the Matrix car park there would be no bother of us getting in. They turned up in their Thames 16 cwt van, just the four of them and Paul was driving. We helped get the gear out of the van, I remember that the drums were partially made-up from the last gig. There were also 2 crates of Newcastle Brown Ale, these were Lennon's pride and joy. Inside John asked if I could play guitar, when I said yes he gave me his Rickenbacker and said "tune the f****r up". I tuned it up with pitch pipes with George and Paul who were also tuning their instruments, while John put on what appeared to be blue eye-shadow. We watched from the wings, and talked to Ringo between numbers, I recall Ringo was not happy with the sound. They were using the house PA". Tracks they probably performed that night include; I Saw Her Standing There and Twist and Shout (these were both definitely performed) Roll over Beethoven, Hippy Hippy Shake, Sweet Little Sixteen, Lend Me Your Comb, Your Feet's Too Big, Mr. Moonlight, Taste of Honey, Kansas City/Hey-Hey-Hey-Hey, Ask Me Why, Red Sails in the Sunset, Everybody's Trying to Be My Baby, Matchbox, I'm Talking About You, Shimmy Shake, and Love Me Do. Jim Twigg of the Tamwoth band The Three Spirits recalls there was a big fight in the club before the Beatles came on stage. Once on though they blew the place apart!

A fifteen-year-old boy from Stoke Heath in Coventry was present at this gig. Not just any old 15 year old, this was Peter Waterman, a boy who would grow up to become one of the country's most influential record producers. It's also interesting to hear that Pete cites this very gig to be a changeling experience for him. It could be argued that this one gig helped shape the career path he would follow; eventually becoming the industry giant he is today. Pete enthuses about this gig in his bestselling autobiography "I Wish, I Was Me" (ISBN 0-7535-0573-8). He talks about them having a blue van with writing all over it, and their Vox amplifiers. Pete tells how he had met them round the pub. The pub in question is the Fletch, on Fletchhamstead Highway. Pete thought that their Liverpool accents were a little hard to decipher, but found them all to be really nice guys, and was impressed by George's Chet Atkins Gretsch 6128 Duo Jet guitar. Once on stage, he tells of how they began their "raw energy" set with "I Saw Her Standing There" dressed in jeans.& quirky jackets to a crowd of around 100 people. So even in their early days Pete Waterman was able to spot the potential talent of the Beatles. Interestingly in the Film "Let It Be" Macca says, "There was some fellow in the front watching how you play". Could that have been Pete Waterman?

Left, there are no pictures of the Beatles at The Matrix (no surprises there), but this one of Jerry Lee Lewis and (Chas &)Dave Peacock may give you a feel of the place. It was taken about 6 months after the Beatles played the venue. Below left the Telegraph cutting & below right the building still has it's original parquet flooring! Bottom right rear of the Matrix changed little since 1962! . Bottom left the support band that night The Mark Allen Group with Lee Terri.

MATRIX HALL, COVENTRY

SATURDAY, NOVEMBER 17th
SCOOP! SCOOP! SCOOP!
Hit Recorders of "Love Me Do."
Direct from their German Tour **THE BEATLES**
With THE MARK ALLEN GROUP - LEE TERI
7.45-11.45 - Licensed Bar - Buffet - Late buses
Tickets 5/6 (6/- at the door)
Tickets available at Jill Hanson's Record Shop, 8, Market Way, Coventry, and The Record Centre, Smithford Way.
SATURDAY, NOVEMBER 24th—For this week only—NO DANCE

Coventry Theatre, February 24th 1963

1962 had been a pretty good year for the Beatles; they had secured a recording contract with EMI, had appeared on TV on four occasions. Then there was the small matter of the first hit single namely "Love Me Do" attaining a number 17 position (or 21 depending on which chart you followed).

So 1963 was shaping up even better and after a brief Scottish tour in January they embarked on their first nationwide tour on February 2nd. Despite the hit record, they remained just another pop band (well at least outside of Merseyside). They would play support to young Helen Shapiro. Helen broke onto the scene in 1961 as a 14 year-old schoolgirl famed for her deep powerful voice. She scored a succession of hits including two number ones "They Don't Know and the classic "Walking Back To Happiness". By 1963 she was virtually an old-timer in show-biz terms (despite only being 17). Her hits would continue throughout 63 but her chart placings were now in double figures, the current hit for this tour "Queen For Tonight" attained just a 33 placing in the hit parade. Ironically as the Beatles fame increased, Helen's seem to be going the other way, a perfect cross-fade of popularity if ever there was one.

Now when I said the Beatles played support to Helen Shapiro, I neglected to mention they were also supporting Danny Williams and Kenny Lynch. Indeed I have a Coventry Theatre advert for the concert before "Please Please Me" charting and The Beatles are not even mentioned on it! A couple of weeks later when "Please Please Me" finally charted the soon to be Fab Four were not only mentioned in the up-dated advert, but referred to as The Dynamic Beatles, and "Please Please Me" is mentioned along side their name. Other acts on the tour were The Kestrels, Red Price Orchestra, The Honeys and comic/host Dave Allan.

The tour had begun with problems, with the Beatles and Helen Shapiro having been barred from a golf club in Carlisle because they had changed from their usual stage-suits back into their casual leather jackets. They never actually made it into the club; the papers apparently had a field day! During a break in the tour the boys recorded their first album "Please Please Me" in a mammoth thirteen-hour session. Two days before the Coventry date, they learnt that their second single "Please Please Me" had hit number one on the NME chart (number 2 in the retail charts).

The NME placing was shared at first with Coventry legend Frank Ifield singing "The Wayward Wind". The day before this concert the boys had made their debut on the TV pop show "Thank Your Lucky Stars. "The show itself saw The Beatles in a buoyant mood following the success of "Please Please Me". Despite Beatlemania not yet being fully on the agenda, the crowd were already screaming and making the concert a noisy affair (as all subsequent Beatles concerts would be).

COVENTRY THEATRE · HALES STREET COVENTRY

Manager G. E. ROBINSON   Telephone 23141

6.0 SUNDAY, 24TH FEB. 8.30 | ONE NIGHT ONLY — TWO PERFORMANCES

ARTHUR HOWES PRESENTS
BRITAIN'S INTERNATIONAL TEENAGE STAR

HELEN SHAPIRO

'LOVE ME DO'
THE DYNAMIC **BEATLES**

SPECIAL GUEST STAR
DANNY WILLIAMS
'MOON RIVER' · 'JEANNIE'

THE KESTRELS
THE HONEYS
THE RED PRICE BAND
DAVE ALLEN

'UP ON THE ROOF'
KENNY LYNCH

SEATS: 8/6 6/6 3/6

programme

This programme is subject to alteration at the discretion of the management

Red Price Band
The Honeys
Dave Allen
The Beatles
(not appearing at Peterborough)
Dave Allen
Danny Williams

INTERVAL

Red Price Band
The Kestrels
Kenny Lynch
Dave Allen
HELEN SHAPIRO

God save the Queen

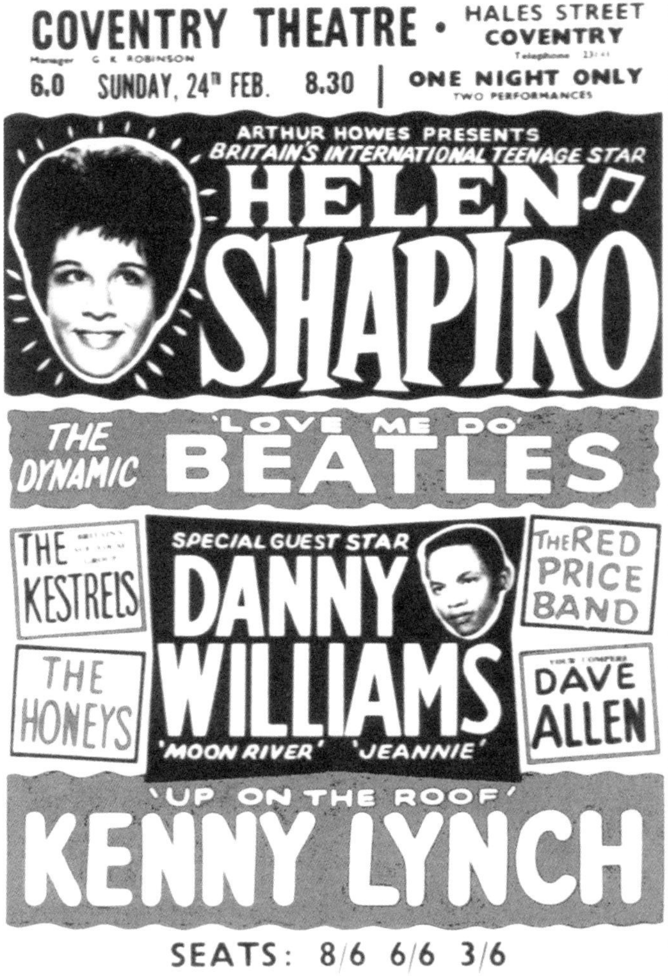

Left, the running order of the show from the original tour programme, note how low down the bill The Beatles were on this tour. *With thanks to Connie Colvin and Julie Maggs.*

Right, the Coventry Theatre poster. *With thanks to Helen Shapiro*

THE COVENTRY THEATRE

Regency Restaurant. Open to the Public for Luncheons Daily. Phone 23143.
Box Office (10 a.m. to 8 p.m.): Cov. 23141 (three lines).

LAST TWO WEEKS — MUST CLOSE MARCH 2nd
Evgs. 7.15 p.m.; Matinees Weds., Thurs., Sats. at 2.45 p.m.
Special Half-term Matinees, Friday, February 22nd and Monday, February 25th.

SIDNEY JAMES
TV's "Citizen James" in Person — In
PUSS IN BOOTS
Also starring
FRANKIE HOWERD
and a Star-studded cast of 70 in Britain's Biggest Pantomime.

4th March (week), Mon.-Fri., 7.15; Mat. Thurs. 2.45. Sat. at 2, 5 and 8 p.m.
MAX BYGRAVES Entertains in his New Show

11th March (week): SADLER'S WELLS OPERA. Repertoire available.
29th March (season): Fabulous SPRING SHOW with KEN DODD, EVE BOSWELL.
Sunday, 24th Feb., 6.0 & 8.30: HELEN SHAPIRO, DANNY WILLIAMS, KENNY LYNCH, The Dynamic BEATLES ("Please Please Me") and other Stars.
Sunday, 3rd Mar., 6.0 & 8.30: JOE BROWN & the "Bruvvers," THE TORNADOS.
Sunday, 10th March, 6.0 & 8.30: FRANK IFIELD and THE SPRINGFIELDS.

The shouting out of the Beatles names during the other performances had also begun and by all accounts the PA sound was particularly abysmal that night. One Nuneaton guy Neil Batchelor got in for free, met all the acts (including The Beatles) and got a full set of autographs, apart from Danny Williams who was on stage at the time. Neil had found a way into the theatre through the costume department. Shortly after getting his autographs, he was rumbled and got thrown out, though he still has the autographs. Pre-gig the Beatles set-up their equipment with Kenny Lynch testing his mike. Meanwhile poor Helen Shapiro tried her best to give an interview between Beatles chords and mike tests. Mercifully Kenny and the boys were soon hauled away for a publicity photo in the circle of the theatre. With Kenny revealing he was about to record a version of the McCartney-Lennon song "Misery".

The Beatles performed the following set at Coventry: Chains, Keep Your Hands Off My Baby, A Taste of Honey and Please, Please Me. They did two performances that night one starting at 6.00 pm and the other at 8.30 pm. The following day the single "Please Please Me" was released onto the American market. I contacted Helen to see if she remembered anything special about the Coventry concert. She remembers the tour but unfortunately not specific dates. She was kind enough to send me a poster of the concert, and sent her regards and best wishes. Helen is now a Messianic Jew and gospel music is now her preferred style, and strangely enough her fan club is based at Strawberry Fields, Meriden near Coventry.

Queuing For Tickets at Coventry, October 14th 1963

Coventry Theatre, November 17th 1963

1963 for the Beatles was tour, tour and tour again, it would represent virtually a whole year on the road, punctuated with recording sessions, TV appearances and interviews. Some nine months had passed since the moptops had graced Coventry with their 'fab' presence, and in the interim Beatlemania had taken a firm hold and they were now happily headlining their own tours. This particular tour was named "The Beatles Autumn Tour 1963" and had begun in Cheltenham on November 1st. The singles "From Me To You" and "She Loves You" had both made number one and "I Want To Hold Your Hand" was about to do the same, not forgetting three chart topping EP's and one chart-topping album. John Lennon had become a Dad and on November 4th they had appeared on the Royal Command Variety Performance (after retiring to a bar at The Mapleton Hotel, *Coventry* St, London). The next day the Daily Mirror's banner headline read Beatlemania!

Consequently, anticipation had been growing in the area for this third and last Coventry Beatles visit. On November 8th it was reported that a letter from a Coventry schoolgirl had been passed to The Lord Mayor Of Coventry. The Stoke Park Schoolgirl had requested that the Beatles should play during school hours so everyone could go and see them. She also mentioned that booking arrangements could take place within the school to avoid truancy. This young lady had obviously never heard the phrase "don't push it", as she also wanted to see the concert for free; suggesting that money spent on tickets could go to charity! Why not just ask the lads to come and play at Stoke Park? Needless to say the Lord Mayor took it all with a pinch of salt.

Mind you she may have had a point, as many had been desperate for tickets. The box office opened at 10.00am 14th October 1963. As to be expected there was a queue of around a thousand people stretching from the Coventry Theatre booking office all the way up to Cook Street Gate. Many had camped out all night; a lot of people in the queue were parents and grandparents who had been persuaded into buying the tickets for young female relations who were at school that day. Not all of them were so noble, some played truant, others had 'gone sick' from work admitting that seeing the Fab Four in the flesh was worth the risk of getting the sack! Those who were waiting all-night got little sleep and spent the winter night dancing and listening to Radio Luxembourg. That too caused the Police to ask them to keep the radios down as they were receiving complaints from the adjacent Fire Station from firemen unable to sleep because of the noise!

When the 4,020 tickets did go on sale they disappeared in a mere four hours. Sadly there was still a queue of 250 fans waiting in vain when the last prize tickets were sold. There was much unhappiness, not least with some of the arrangements. Many punters were buying tickets for both performances and despite the four tickets per person rule some bought as many as thirty!

Above, the Beatles play Scalextrix in the backstage bar at the Coventry Theatre. Below The Beatles on stage in Coventry.
Photographs courtesy of Mirror Syndication International

Tickets, by the way, were priced at 12/6, 10/6 & 8/- (for the Stalls "Jewellery Rattlers") 10/6 &8/-(Circle) and 6/- (The Upper Circle "The Cheap Seats").

So on 17th November (exactly one year to the day of their first Coventry visit at the Matrix 17th November 1962-spooky or what. To add to the spookiness The Rolling Stones had played in Coventry at The Matrix the day before on 16-11-63) The Beatles circus came to town for those lucky enough to own tickets. Three girls, who were unable to obtain tickets, purchased them for the Saturday Birthday Show then hid in the toilets. How they thought they could hide for some eighteen hours between shows, demonstrates just what a hold these four 'scousers' had on people. Sadly the girls were rumbled well in advance of the show and they never got to see their idols.

The Police officer in charge of "Operation Beatle" Superintendent E. Townsend was taking no chances as far as Beatle security went. "Everyone was expecting gimmicks", he told the Coventry Evening Telegraph at the time, "So we went the other way and brought them in by the most direct route". The Beatles had left their Hotel at The Branksome Towers near Bournemouth late morning, stopping en route for a spot of lunch, before phoning ahead to Coventry Police station for further instructions. One of the police requirements was that they arrived at 3.30pm, before school ended. According to the Coventry Evening Telegraph they missed the deadline by 30 minutes and got into Coventry at 4.00pm.

On arrival in Coventry they travelled in their Austin Princess car from Little Park Street Police Station, down Hight St into Broadgate onto the Burges and then Hales Street straight into the back of the Coventry Theatre. Almost immediately barriers went up behind the car to protect the group from the 200 or so girls who had braved the winter rain to see their idols! Beatles road manager Neil Aspinall, was happy with Superintendent Townsend's handling of it all. Back stage the guys spent the time playing Scalextrix (the slot car racing game). Paul was showing no side effects of his recent bout of gastric flu that saw the Portsmouth show on the 11th cancelled. He told the Coventry press "he was the weak anaemic one, according to one newspaper because I was ill last week. I'm actually fine now, (a few days before the concert fans were so worried about the 'doe-eyed one's ill health that the national press was giving hour by hour bulletins of his recovery). Lennon was his usual acerbic self and interjected," Now everyone is waiting for us to crack up under the strain, I'll tell you this. When we are breaking down we'll make a public announcement so everyone can come and take pictures".

Actress Julie Christie, who was appearing in Billy Liar in Birmingham, was also back stage, eager to meet the boys, and a drum kit was presented to Jean Owen of the Vernon girls as a birthday present from Ringo and the Beatles for her 20th. Much of the time though was spent talking to the press; the big concern was items thrown on the stage, particularly jelly babies (this ritual began when George mentioned that Ringo kept stealing his jelly babies). George complained, "We've had jelly babies thrown at us by the hundred, something hit me in the eye last night, one of us will be getting hurt". Tonight it got worse when Ringo got hit in the head with a woman's shoe. The next day Brian Epstein publicly asked fans to stop throwing gifts and jelly babies. Sadly the message never got across and when they went to America they were greeted with jellybeans rather than jelly babies, and they were even harder.

During the show many girls kept vigils outside, passing gifts to policewomen at the stage door. These included letters, chocolate, a basket of fruit and a hand knitted Beatle doll, with special letters for the guys secreted upon it. One fan, John Read, sent the crowd outside wild, when heading for his seat in gods, he spotted a small open window put his hand out and waved. The crowd apparently went wild thinking it was one of the Beatles! Vi Cox and Carol Gillespie, are two ladies who still remember having no tickets but still waiting in the rain during the show. "I remember it pouring down and I had pinched and eventually broke my sister's umbrella," Admits Vi. "We were all screaming and people were fainting, we were about 13 at the time, there were about six of us, all school friends from Cardinal Wiseman School.

"We had had arranged at school to meet up at Coventry Theatre on the Sunday", Carol remembers, "Everyone was so excited. We all talked about it at school. But no one could afford to go in. We didn't really even get to see them, we were told they were driven away dressed as policemen (this was not the case as pictures show. This policemen event actually happened in Birmingham few days earlier on the 11th November).

Not all of those gathered were Beatles fans, there was a rival gang of Peter Jay and The Jaywalkers fans present. On the subject of Peter Jay, I asked Jaywalkers guitarist Pete Miller if he had any recollections of the Coventry concert. His reply was to the point," When you eat a can of peas, you don't know which one makes you fart! Coventry was just another night on a seemingly endless cycle of one nighters. However there were a few nice birds outside the stage door. I remember that cus' I actually met up with one of them again last year".

First on stage were The Kestrels (who included Tony Burrows and Roger Greenaway, who released a non-charting cover of the Lennon-McCartney song 'There's A Place"). Followed by Peter Jay and the Jay Walkers (Peter Jay was the drummer, they charted at 31 with the single "Can Can 62"). The Vernon Girls followed (Sponsored by the Liverpool pools company Vernons. They began as a 70-piece choir. They had a hit in Canada with the song "We Love The Beatles" and the UK hits, Lover Please and "You Know What I mean").

Comedian Frank Berry was the host of the show and favoured the "putting out a fire with gasoline approach" It wasn't enough for him that the crowd was already a mass of hyperventilating pre-pubescents. Mr Berry's trick was to come to the microphone and announce "And now from Liverpool we have......"The Vernon Girls". Oh how The Vernon ' stage lighting, Bert Royle, added to the hysteria by projecting a slide of the Fab Four on to the curtains in advance of their arrival.

The Brook Brothers took the stage next (Ricky and Geoff, real-life brothers who

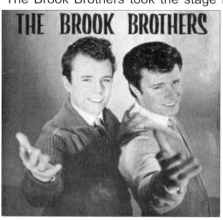

had hits with "War paint" and "Ain't Gonna Wash For A Week"). All the acts would have to put up with chants of "We Want The Beatles" throughout their sets. When the Beatles finally arrived on stage, it was of course pandemonium; John, Paul, George and Ringo were wearing dark suits with black velvet collars. John with his Rickenbacker 325, George playing a Gretsch Country Gentleman guitar and Paul was playing his trademark Hofner violin bass and of course Ringo at the back on his Ludwig drums. The stage was sparse by today's standards, draped curtains, two mics and a tiny back-line of vox amplifiers (though the newspaper report at the time described them as a "battery of amplifiers" (goodness knows what he would have made of Deep Purple's or the Grateful Dead's back-line?) Needless to say, the amplification could not compete with the hoards of screaming fans. Many fans became hysterical, some even collapsing. The St John Ambulance Brigade had their work cut out that night, many fans ran to the front of the upper circle dangerously waving at the mop tops, oblivious of any dangers (I wonder if they tell their grandchildren about what they got up to!)

The set list for the night looked like this. "I Saw Here Standing There", "From Me To You", All My Loving", You Really Got A Hold Of me", "Boys", "Till There Was You", "She Loves You", "Money" and "Twist and Shout". Apparently "She Loves You" and "Twist And Shout" were the two songs that were greeted with more enthusiasm than the others in the set (if that was at all possible). None of it could be heard of course, Paul, when asked about the screaming figured, "the fans paid for the concert so it was up to them if they wanted to scream. He did admit it was a shame for the fans who just wanted to listen to the music (he probably meant male fans there)! By all accounts the audience at the second performance were better behaved and road manager Neil Aspinall said that the Coventry crowds were overall better behaved that at many other theatres. The Fab Four were whisked away directly after the second performance. Standing at the stage door was Mrs. Nan Egginton, the stage door keeper (she had earlier shared a pot of tea with the Fab Four). Apparently the getaway was done so fast that most fans never ever saw the car leave. A policewoman sat in the passenger seat next to the chauffeur as they sped back to the police station, then on to their overnight hotel at Brooklands Farm. While this was going on fans were still outside the Coventry Theatre convinced that their idols were still inside. One very upset young lady saw the car but refused to accept is was The Beatles because there were no guitars in it! Oh dear! Next day the Fabaroonies had a concert-free day and left for London to be guests of honour at EMI House, where they received silver disc awards for sales of the albums "Please Please Me" and "With The Beatles".

SUNDAY 17th NOVEMBER at 6.0 and 8.30 p.m.

THE BEATLES

THE BROOK BROTHERS

PETER JAY
AND THE JAYWALKERS

THE KESTRELS

ADVANCE BOOKING COMMENCES
FOR PERSONAL APPLICANTS ONLY
ON 14th OCTOBER

Stalls : 12/6, 10/6, 8/- Circle : 10/6, 8/- U/Circle, 6/-

John shares a cuppa with Coventry Theatre's stage door keeper Mrs Nan Eggington while Paul chats to actress Julie Christie. Above Coventry Theatre paraphernalia.

Main photograph courtesy of Mirror Syndication International

From small acorns does mighty art grow

1968 was shaping up as a turbulent year, Martin Luther King and Robert Kennedy had both been assassinated, and widespread rioting was becoming the norm. It was no surprise then that The Beatles and in particular John Lennon would look for a far more serene solution, in the shape of a World Peace campaign.

John and Yoko had "just" become an item, in that instance they created an artistic "dynamic" that would astound and often infuriate the popular press. Lennon was the creative genius looking for a new way to use his talents. Yoko was the ultimate "thinking" artist and would become the creative conduit to help take John's new ideas down a sometimes off-centre and surrealistic path. Despite their art being considered eccentric in the extreme it would always be executed in the name of a higher cause. More often than not that higher cause was world peace. Well so it was on 15th June 1968, John with Yoko Ono (mid way through recording *The White Album*, between the tracks *Blackbird* & *Revolution 9* to be exact) attended 'The National Sculpture Exhibition' in the grounds of Coventry Cathedral.

This was to be the couple's first 'real' time out in public together and first joint artistic venture, entitled '*Acorns For Peace,* or *Living Art-Two Acorns*, (they would later name-check acorns in the Beatles song *Ballad of John and Yoko,* when Lennon sings, "Fifty acorns tied in a sack"). As Coventry Cathedral was (and still is) a dominion of reconciliation and world peace, it was an obvious place for the couple to "perform" their peace-art. They turned up in John's long white Rolls Royce (with very advanced features for 1968 including TV, video recorder, 'floating' record player and Telephone). On the back was attached a trailer (a perfect example of Lennon's paradoxical life-style). On the trailer was a round white circular metal seat of two halves that when pushed together formed a circle. The intention was to sit on and contemplate the growing of the acorns beneath you. Natural art if you like. What could be more perfect than that? They would plant two acorns (in white plastic cups) in the centre of it, with one facing East, and one West, symbolising the meeting of John & Yoko, and their two different cultures. The day however was filled with problems. First the couple's sculpture was banned from being shown in the main exhibit area in the ruins of the old Cathedral. Fabio Barraclough, who was the assistant of art at Rugby School and the chief organiser of the event, claimed that it was Canon Stephen Verney who had the sculpture moved because he objected to exhibiting their work on consecrated ground because of their extra-marital relationship.

Canon Stephen Verney later refuted this claim. He was unhappy however about this metal bench and acorns being considered 'art' and the fact the couple had signed up for the exhibition at the last minute. Probably because of that John and

Yoko's exhibit was not mentioned in the main catalogue, so they produced their own, (basically one sheet folded making 4 pages, with a thin tissue paper cover but even this was not allowed to be distributed. (So I'm really happy to actually own a copy of the said catalogue). In the privacy of the Deanery, Yoko became hysterical and was shouting at the Canon to ring leading artists (including Henry Moore who was not at home) to prove that their work was indeed 'art'!

Me and my original catalogue from 1968, fully signed by Yoko Ono (see right) & Anthony Fawcett, proudly sat in front of the Cathedral backdrop photo taken by Keith McMillan.
Inside it says "This is what happens when clouds meet" John Lennon. This is what happens when clouds meet" (the piece is John's idea but it was so good that I stole it) Yoko Ono.

Anthony Fawcett's words from the programme.

'John -Yoko' at Coventry

The concept of these sculptures by John Lennon and Yoko Ono is expressed by their statement 'this is what happens when two clouds meet'. It is symbolic and humorous at the same time. The thoughts behind it are beautiful and it's true fulfilment through the cycle of growth is an end in itself-the best idea that can ever be conceived as a work of art —mother nature is supreme, overriding man's artificial constructions.

The seeds, although they cannot be seen at this stage, are acorns and slowly the oak trees will develop. It covers all fields for them-it's a game, a joke, but at the same time serious, in the idiom of their music, their writings or even. These ideas place them on a higher level than other sculptures in the exhibition so they need to be looked at through new eyes. Cry, laugh, or walk into the sky. There will never be another like them.

The actual planting was to take just a few minutes, with John spading the turf and digging a hole a foot square. When East and West had been properly deduced, the pots were laid in their correct positions and covered with earth. After a few words from John describing what the acorns represented it was all over. The couple were soon in the 'Roller' and on their way back to Surrey. Anthony Fawcett recalls in his fascinating book John Lennon: One Day At A Time, how John had remained calm through it all until he was back in the privacy of his car and became enraged at the treatment he felt he had received.

After the couple had left the seat, the acorns were inexplicably moved from in front of the Chapel of Unity across to the Cathedral gardens (about 50 foot). A spokesperson at the time said it was because it looked better there. I find this inexplicable action hard to understand. Here we have one of the world's greatest musical icons, and no matter what anyone else felt, this to him and Yoko was a work of art, it was important to them. Then you get someone almost on a whim deciding the whole thing looked better elsewhere! Would that same person have tampered with the Mona Lisa's hair because they felt she would look better blonde? I can only apologise as a Coventrian that such a mindless act occurred in my city of birth.

It was all academic, however, because within a few days the acorns and the plaque on the sculpture were stolen (if E-bay had been around then, one wonders how many hundreds of supposedly genuine 'peace' acorns would have been up for sale?). *The Coventry Telegraph* even got an anonymous call from someone claiming to be the acorn thief. The myths of that Saturday in June continue. Some say the couple were so upset they later sent some more acorns and they were put under 24 hour security (or armed guard as one US site claims). Some say they never sent replacements. Staff at the Cathedral believed the trees grew for some 25 years then died. Certainly there seems to be no sign of this in their original position. There is a school of thought that suggests that if replacements had been planted we probably wouldn't have been privy to it .

The bench/sculpture itself was later removed by Lennon's chauffeur Les Anthony and taken back down to Kenwood on the trailer. John and Yoko are seen sitting on it briefly in the film Imagine (actually an extract from Yoko's film "Rape"). In 1984 when Strawberry Fields was opened in Central Park New York. Yoko mentioned that sixteen years earlier she and John had planted acorns in the precincts of Coventry Cathedral. That acorn was now symbolically a tree. So no matter what happened to those two little acorns, the Cathedral at Coventry is an important part of the John and Yoko story. It's worth pointing out that Coventry Cathedral was chosen by the couple because of its credo as a centre for world peace and reconciliation. The fact that the then Canon took this 'pop star' art with a pinch of salt has little bearing on the all-embracing work that 'our' Cathedral has undertaken over the years.

The event although somewhat negative at the time, has now taken on a life of it's own. In June 2005 the 37th anniversary of the John and Yoko visit, I dedicated my weekly Backbeat page in the Coventry Evening Telegraph to the story. Much of the text here is based on the feature; in closing I wrote these prophetic words.

"Both sides seem to look on it as a just a piece of history now, I may be off-track here, but wouldn't it be wonderful to have Yoko and Sean Lennon unveil some symbolic brass acorns at the Cathedral and give peace a chance once more"! I actually sent the text of the article off to Yoko Ono in New York. I never heard anything back, but few months later, I got a phone-call from Pete Walters of CV One and I learnt that Yoko was to make a return visit to the Cathedral. It was incredible news. Had I influenced the trip? Who knows; what I do know is that it was hell living with that secret for such a length of time. Obviously those who knew were sworn to secrecy, "letting the Yoko out of the bag" would have ruined everything. Because of my involvement I was VIP listed for the event, my main wish was to meet Yoko and get a photograph with her. I was also very keen to show her my Coventry Evening Telegraph article; of course I was fully prepared for an army of bodyguards, what actually happened is revealed in the next chapter....Before we go there there's the matter of a certain letter (see page 27).

A somewhat 'rattled' Lennon put pen to paper about his and Yoko's treatment thirteen days after their return. Interestingly The Beatles, and more specifically Lennon, were working on the track "Everybody's Got something To Hide Except Me and My Monkey". The song was about the couple of course. In 1980 John admitted that he wrote it feeling that everyone was getting paranoid, except him and Yoko, no doubt his visit to Coventry only helped to endorse that fact!

Left, the original bench from 1968, in it's second location in the Cathedral Gardens, not Unity Gardens where John & Yoko originally placed it . Below the 2005 version. *Photo of the original bench courtesy of Mirror Syndication International*

The Lennon Letter. 28th June 1968

Dear Cannon Verney

Thank you for your <u>Christians</u> attitude. I think the leaflet is explicit-Anthony Fawcett's notes are especially for 'puzzled people'-anyway do you have to explain an acorn? I <u>don't</u> understand why you can't issue our leaflet unless you worry about gossips (cast the first stone etc). The Christian Church does allow divorce doesn't it? Christians are supposed to stand for TRUTH. Christ stood for people-Yoko and I are people.-Of course the piece is about Yoko and me,-it's also about <u>you</u> and me, and anyone else you care to mention-it's about EVERYONE and EVERYTHING. You talk about young people as if you know something about them-you obviously don't or you wouldn't be worried about <u>our</u> influence on them.

Jesus would have loved our piece for what it is

* Love John Lennon

PS Could we not substitute something which is not worth stealing instead of Coventry Cathedral, and which says quite simply. "Sit here, and think of a church growing into a bigger church."-Then we needn't bother to have clergy and everyone can enjoy <u>THE</u> idea.
* ♡

Needless to say that we have all moved on, Yoko's second visit to the Coventry proved that, as did the reception she received at the Cathedral. Even John dug it, up in the clouds high above our heads.

Some John & Yoko/Coventry trivia.

The Acorns for Peace idea would be pursued in 1969 when the couple sent various world leaders acorns to plant for peace. It would seem most of them ignored the plea except for Golda Meir of Israel and Pierre Trudeau of Canada!

On arrival at Coventry, in 1968 John and Yoko were mobbed by autograph hunters, Lennon was happy to oblige although Yoko appeared nervous. A small reception was held in the Cathedral's restaurant for the famous visitors.

There is a large picture display of John and Yoko at Coventry Cathedral at The John Lennon Museum in Saitama, Japan.

A Picture of John & Yoko planting the acorns in Coventry formed part of a free calendar given away with the "Live Peace From Toronto" Album by the Plastic Ono Band.

Despite the ceremony taking place in June, the plaque actually reads "Yoko" by John Lennon, "John" by Yoko Ono, Some time in May 1968. The seat was insured for £4,500!

While the Isle of Wight Pop Festival was taking place In the summer of 1970. A rock concert of a much smaller scale was happening in the ruins of Coventry Cathedral. "The Diggers Feast" was probably a gesture of reconciliation to what had transpired with John & Yoko in 1968. It was organised by the Coventry 'Diggers', a Hippie-like movement named after the 'Levellers' of the 1600's. Incidentally John Lennon had once brought an Island (Dorinish) for the national movement of 'Diggers' off the West coast of Ireland.

Top Coventry Beatle fan Steve Rouse, with just some of his vast Beatle collection including the calendar showing John & Yoko in Coventry that came free with the "Live Peace From Toronto" LP.

Yoko's Return October 14th 2005

So it was on Friday that Yoko Ono came back to our City and continued the work she and John Lennon had begun some 37 years and 4 months previously. As part of Coventry Peace Month she dedicated two Japanese oak trees in the Cathedral gardens.

As preparations for her arrival took place, I got to thinking that the scene that had occurred over 37 years previously had now been allowed out of it's 'freeze frame state' and the film had finally been left to run. You see when I first researched the John & Yoko visit for my book Godiva Rocks and Backbeat column, the whole experience had echoed like a ghost from the past, it was just a piece of local music history. I recall the day when my wife Julie and I stood in the Cathedral grounds, with various photos in our hands locating the exact position of where the bench/acorns had been. Most people ignored us, a few people stared, but it seemed like out of the whole world only myself and Julie had any interest in what we were doing. At a later date we actually moved the repro-bench to the Cathedral to take pictures for the Telegraph article. The feeling was much the same, it's worth mentioning that we had nothing but help from Coventry Cathedral and they even assisted in moving the bench. Yes it was a lonely moment, a glimpse of the past, just something that occurred nearly forty years ago, pretty much forgotten. That was until Yoko came once again to finish the job and help show how we have all moved on. Suddenly the world wants to see the bench and hear the story of the visit.

When Yoko arrived though, all those lost years seemed to disappear. This time it went like clockwork and Pete Walters and his CV One team Jo Hibbard and her Cathedral team deserve a huge pat on the back for yet another job performed superbly for the city. The day was not particularly bright, but at least the predictable English rain stayed away that afternoon. At around 3.30 she arrived, without any bodyguards, just a team of very helpful aids, including Murray Chalmers, her very charming and professional press officer.

The ceremony itself held on Unity Lawn included a welcome from the then Lord Mayor Cllr Ram Lakah (and in my opinion the best Lord Mayor we ever had), and the present Dean Of Coventry, The Very Rev John Irvine (a true man of the people). Yoko symbolically un-knotted a silken rope wrapped around both of the already planted oak tree saplings.

Yoko Unties the rope, watched by Cllr Lakah.
Photo by Hannah Tobin

Top left The Ceremony with Pete Walters of CV One, Yoko, The Dean Of Coventry and the Lord Mayor of Coventry. Top right the new bench festooned with oak trees. The other four photos are the author with Yoko , presenting a 2-Tone Trail badge, and Yoko graciously signing the original 1968 programme.

Yoko addressed the gathering, and said, "It's a great honour to be here today and to be here at the beginning of the month of peace. In 1968 John and I sat close to this very spot and this was to be the first of many peace events we did. It is great to be back here 37 years later to continue something we started here. John would have loved it."

Children from the city's Southfields Primary School sang "Come on All Children", and two youngsters Shannon Bayliss and Tom Lockhart read out the words to the John & Yoko song "Grow Old With Me". Yoko seemed to be more than happy to be there and handed out acorns to many of the children present. (After the event oak trees were distributed to every school in Coventry). During the press interviews, Yoko revealed how happy she was to be back in Coventry, how great the city was doing this, mentioning how she remembered the last time she was there, then quite wisely moved on to say that it was significant she was invited back, believing it was her fate and John's fate that she was here again. Central TV reporter Yvonne Gaskill asked what John would have thought if he had been here today, Yoko replied, "he would have loved it, he would have said we are here again, I think he is with us today."

Once the main press pack had had their time with Japan's most famous person (who was still sat on the bench) it was my turn to show her my Backbeat piece and read her the fact that I had suggested a visit as far back as June. "In June" she replied, "I didn't know that then, I didn't even know I was coming ". She seemed genuinely surprised by the prophetic angle of it all. I then produced the original and very rare catalogue from their visit in 1968. "Remember this" I asked, "Of course I do" she replied, "You have the original" she said. I asked her to sign it, and to my delight she did. She wrote on it, **"To Pete love Yoko 2005. PS Imagine Peace!** No my friends it's not for sale. Indeed even before it was signed it had attracted bags of attention and was even featured on Central TV 's news coverage of the event.

Above, Anthony Fawcett reads his original words from the 1968 programme.

Anthony Fawcett (right) and the author.

I was lucky enough to talk to her again later at the reception in the Deanery, after her last visit here she left red faced and angry over the way her and John's art had been treated. This time by marked contrast it was tea and canapés all round. As I had a new book about Coventry's 2-Tone about to hit the shops I presented Yoko with a 2-Tone Tra badge. She seemed to have heard of The Specials and I believe that John Lennon once sourced a Selecter record to show studio musicians the kind of sound he wanted and he liked the band Madness. Two Tone also took up a lot of the racial unity ideals that John and Yoko cared about so much, showing yet another positive side of our city, the City of Peace & Reconciliation. I found Yoko to be courteous and obliging, putting up with all the pushing and shoving and attention she received throughout her time with us. Yet she still seems to have become a 'bad-press' magnet. We yes she married an icon, but does anyone seriously still believe she was the catalyst for the Beatles split? It's all history now anyway, so forget it and move on!

Also present in 1968 was Anthony Fawcett, and to my delight he was also there today. A charming man who became like an unofficial minister of Art for the couple, his role in the art world today is immense. He wrote the original text on the 1968 catalogue and was delighted to see my copy and read his words once again. Anthony too kindly signed it. His memories of that day formed part of his insightful book One Day At A Time.

So as the circle comes complete, it's worth reflecting on what the event was about. Reconciliation, peace, harmony, the coming together of East and West and with a return from Yoko promised to oversee the inauguration of the plaque. With this in mind is it not time we seized the day and introduced an Acorns For Peace Foundation in the city, possibly funding peace projects and educational musical courses in Coventry?

Kozue Etsuzen, London representative of the John Lennon Museum, Japan

When Yoko Ono returned to Coventry in 2005, the John Lennon Museum in Japan was planning the new exhibition called "Love And Peace Activities By John And Yoko". It was a wonderful surprise to all of us in the museum. The original Acorn Event was naturally going to be the biggest feature, but we can also feature something happening at the present time, leading into the future.

didn't personally speak to Yoko about Coventry but the city must be a special place in her mind. The 2005 Acorn Event is significant in two ways. One, you can call it the first work by John and Yoko in years. In the first decade or so after John's passing, Yoko's priority seemed to be solely on John and his work, rather than her own, or even John and Yoko's. In recent years, she has become much more active in her own art. Now she is working on what the Lennon's did as a couple – to kick start, she went back to the very first work they did together, finishing the unfinished project. What a marvelous idea The other, the new acorn trees will be a bridge between the two cities in the East and the West.

Yoko grew up during the Second World War and the experience had a significant impact on her life and work. Hiroshima resurrected itself after the devastating destruction by the bomb as Coventry did by the Blitz. And both cities are looking forward – working towards "Peace and Reconciliation." I am certain that Yoko feels the connection between the two cities. With her 2005 visit to Coventry, things seem to have come to the full circle for her. John would have been proud. It is a blessing to see two trees growing for love and peace in a city of peace.

Above the new oak trees and temporary plaque, right Yoko on the bench.

Yoko's return, as seen through the eyes of the man who helped organise the event, CV One's Pete Walters

The phone call was pretty much to the point. "Hello Pete. I met Yoko Ono in New York the other day. How would you like her to come and plant some trees in the grounds of Coventry Cathedral?" The voice belonged to Bob Eaton, Coventry-based writer and theatre director. And I didn't need to be asked twice. Yoko returning now would set at rest the misunderstandings that followed the visit that she and John Lennon made to the cathedral in 1968. As an influential figure in the global peace movement, her support would be invaluable in our efforts to make more of Coventry's profile as a place that has taken peace and reconciliation seriously. And the trees would in time become a visitor attraction in their own right.

We put together a small team to find a site in the cathedral grounds, source the trees themselves – two three-metre high Japanese oaks – and plan an event that we were sure would capture the media's attention. Over the next twelve weeks many details and suggestions sailed backwards and forwards over the Atlantic by email. Yoko wanted a silken rope linking the trees that she could symbolically untie when the moment came. It was decided that children from Southfields School in Coventry would sing and read words by John and Yoko and that every school in the city would receive an oak sapling to plant in celebration of the event. In due course there would be a stone plaque set into the ground as a permanent reminder of Yoko's visit.

The news finally broke the day before. As we'd hoped, it attracted plenty of media interest and there was a satisfyingly large scrum of reporters and cameramen on hand as Yoko walked up the Queen's steps and into the cathedral precincts, a diminutive figure in a dark suit and white cap, dwarfed by the huge columns of the porch. The next hour seemed to pass in a blur. The Lord Mayor and senior clergy were warmly welcoming, the children from Southfields sang lustily and Yoko was friendliness itself, signing autographs and doing interview after interview with a smile that never wavered. And then it was onto the Dean's house before a final brief guided tour of the cathedral ruins, pausing to read the Japanese inscription on the striking 'Reconciliation' sculpture that symbolises so much the work of the cathedral. As Yoko's long white limousine bore her away, it felt as though the wounds of the past had truly healed and that maybe this was the beginning of a genuine friendship for the future, based on mutual respect. Yoko will be back to see the stone plaque commemorating that afternoon in October, 2005, and her visit has already opened up a new relationship with the John Lennon Museum in Japan, who now have a corner of their exhibition hall that is forever Coventry.

An A to Z of Coventry-Beatles Connections

OK here's a collection of various Beatle connections there are in the area of Coventry and district. We begin with The Beatles' Coventry, looking at various places in the area you may be able to soak up a little Beatle vibe!

Coventry Theatre on her last days. *Photo by Hannah Tobin*

The Beatles' Coventry

Looking for somewhere to soak up some Beatle-vibe in Coventry and area has become a harder job since the 'ultimate' Beatle place in Coventry, namely The Coventry Theatre was torn down. The site of the theatre is at the northern foot of the spectacular Whittle Arch, in front of the equally spectacular Coventry Transport Museum. Now home to the non-spectacular Millennium clock.

1. Brooklands Farm
Now The Brooklands Grange Hotel and Restaurant, Holyhead Road, Coventry.
This one could have gone into "The Think For Yourself" section. It is accepted by many local Beatles fans to be the Hotel the Moptops rested their er..moptops after their November 1963 gig at Coventry Theater. This fact is used on the hotel advertising, as is rumour that if you listen very hard during a visit, you can hear the voice of John Lennon in the Corridors. The present owners are to change all that as they are unsure that the boys ever stayed here. Though there is no smoke without fire. In November 1963 the word got about to fans that this is where they would stay. The then manager Fredrick Tyler told the Coventry Express, "We must have has 150 phone calls asking for tickets, why should they pick on us I don't know. The Beatles are not staying here, In fact I don't think they are staying in Coventry on Sunday night". One gang of teenagers threatened to camp out on the hotels grounds until they were given tickets! The Manager seemed to be well informed of the Beatles movements though, and if they were stopping there he was hardly going to advertise the fact was he?

2. Coventry Cathedral
Coventry City Centre
Probably the most tangible and unchanged Beatle site in the city. The area is shown on page 23. The two new oak trees are located here, and Yoko will return as some point when a commemorative stone plaque is unveiled. The Cathedral is a pleasant place to be on a balmy summer's day. Walk down St Michael's Avenue and let your mind drift back to June 1968. With images of John and Yoko both in white, spades in hand digging the Cathedral turf, and planting their precious acorns.

3. Coventry Theatre *Hales Street*
My introduction really says it all, but there is still a vibe of sorts to be had, Head for the Coventry Transport Museum, before you get to the entrance head right Turn the corner under the blue walk-way steps and you will come to Chauntry Place. Go just inside and this side of the brick wall (before you get to the houses on the other side) is where the stage door of the theatre was located. Although the area has changed radically, this part certainly has echoes of the past. You can imagine the boys frantically running out of the stage exit, straight into their car.

Above left Paul and Cov fan Carolyne Helme
Above right "John-Yoko-Acorns", an oil on canvas by Lynn Clarke, based on the couple's visit to the Cathedral. Below the Boys leave the Theatre watched by stage door keeper Mrs Nan Eggington. Right former owners of the Brookland Farm Hotel Robert & Lesley Jackson, bottom Coventry Theatre. *Top & Bottom Photographs courtesy of Mirror Syndication International*

4. Matrix
Fletchamstead Highway
Now a HSS Hire shop, (see page 10), run by a good team of friendly guys who knew of the buildings history, and were kind enough to show us the original flooring and the area where the stage was originally was located.

The Matrix Building

The Fletch pub

Above, this is the route the fab four would have taken to walk from the Matrix to the Fletch. So when did Macca get his speeding ticket?

Left
The Fletch.

Above the Beatles swap some chord shapes with Actress Julie Christie on stage at Coventry Theatre November 17th 1963. Below The Fab Four on stage at Coventry Theatre November 17th 1963. *Photographs courtesy of Mirror Syndication International*

5. Fletch
Fletchamstead Highway
This was the pub where music legends to be Pete Waterman and The Beatles shared a drink, probably to cool the nerves, judging by Paul's comments on this gig from the Let It Be film. Being just a few yards from the Matrix, this was a regular watering whole for Matrix musicians and punters alike. Most of the inside has changed and a little of the outside, but much of the pub's character is thankfully intact. This was also the area where Macca picked up a speeding ticket on July 22nd 1968! (see page 48).

6. Nuneaton Co-op Hall
Queens Road, Nuneaton
Still pretty much unchanged outside from that legendary night in October 1962 when John, Paul, George, and Ringo came to the Midlands for the first time. Now a monument of neglect, with the hall occasionally used for gigs and the lower area a supermarket. There's no evidence of course but it's fair to assume that the guys would have probably taken themselves off to The Nags Head just up the Queens Road for a little pre-gig drink.

7. Clifton Hall
Near Clifton Upon Dunsmore village
The house has been given much TLC and is now a private (note the word) residence. So no trespassing please.

And just for fun...for those of you who are easily pleased you could try to get some Beatles vibes in the following places..............
Strawberry Fields in Meriden
Lennon Close and Harrison Close in Hillmorton Nr Rugby
Abbey Road, in Whitley Coventry (see below)
Harrison Crescent in Bedworth
Pepper Lane in central Coventry (there's no street sign there now).

This is Abbey Road Coventry style, no studio or zebra crossing. Though it was home in the 80's to Horace Panter, bassman extraordinaire with the 2-Tone band The Specials.

And now the A-to Z……………..

Clifton Hall

Long before there was Fame Academy there was Clifton Hall Pop School, run by manager/promoter music guru Reg Calvert. Reg was no ordinary manager, his style was unorthodox to say the least, but he always brought home the bacon. Clifton Hall was East of the Warwickshire Town of Rugby. An ideal central location from where he could send his various 'acts' out from to venues all over the country. The place was a magnet for visiting pop and rock stars and they were always made welcome. "Lots of people came to Clifton Hall", reveals Reg's daughter Sue Moore, "The Beatles visited Clifton Hall but they didn't sleep there. Lots of famous people came up to the house and, some stayed if they were between gigs. No one ever paid to stay - they just fitted in and found a bed! It was very relaxed. Girls and girlfriends were not allowed to stay. The house was also alcohol and drug free. (Drugs were hardly used in the early 1960's by any of the groups that we knew.)"

Clifton Hall, with thanks to Susan Moore

Tony Clarke was a Coventry kid who spent a lot of time at Clifton Hall with a band called The Atlantics. He recalls Jerry Lee Lewis visiting Clifton, picking up a guitar (not an instrument you normally equate with Lewis) and jamming along with Tony on bass. He also remembers a life-changing moment when John Lennon was there. "He told me that I should embrace music completely, Make it your life, go for it, we have opened the door for new bands now get in there". The words were heeded, and a little later Tony had produced his first chart hit "Mirror, Mirror" for Rugby (and Reg Calvert) band "Pinkerton's Assorted Colours. Tony went on to be a top-flight producer and produced all the classic Moody Blues albums, including the track "Nights In White Satin", he also produced "Simple Game" for The Four Tops.

A rare photo of Jerry Lee Lewis with guitar.

Happy Nat

Nat "rubber-neck" Jackley Actually born in Sunderland in 1909, but this 'physical' comedian (he could twist his neck to give the effect it was made of rubber) lived in Styvechale, Coventry for many, many years. Began his career in a clog dance troupe The 8 Lancashire Lads (a certain Charlie Chaplin was once a member). He was to star in his own show "Nat's In the Belfrey" in 1956. His odd voice and looks won him many small character parts through his long career. Including cameos in the films Yanks and Mrs Brown You've Got a Lovely Daughter, and also on TV in Minder and Juliet Bravo.

However it was his appearance in The Beatles "Magical Mystery Tour" as Happy Nat (the rubber man) for which he will be best remembered. Apparently John was a big Nat Jackley fan, and actually directed Nat personally during one MMT scene. Nat went on the record saying how nice all the Beatles were to him during filming of the magical Mystery Tour. Nat died in Coventry September 1988.

He's Got The Devil In His Heart

The Satanist/author and teacher of the dark Aleister Crowley was born in Leamington Spa (near Coventry) on 12th October 1875. He referred to himself as *The Beast* (popularising the phrase 666, The number of The Beast) His influence is far and wide, none more so in the world of rock music. Led Zeppelin (and in particular) Jimmy Page had a deep interest in him. Page actually owned Crowley's former house *Bolskine* on the banks of Loch Ness. Those reverse speech 'freaks' who play records backward claim Stairway To Heaven is riddled with Crowley inspired satanic messages. Ozzy Osbourne wrote and recorded the song *Mr Crowley*. Iron Maiden sang *The Number of the Beast* and even The Beatles included Crowley on their Sgt Pepper cover (he's the bald headed gentleman, second one in from the Left top row). Of course the Internet is littered with sites claiming the Beatles are the anti-Christ, because of John's "Bigger Than Christ" remarks and because Crowley features on the Pepper's Cover. They say John said, "The whole Idea of The Beatles was based on Crowley's "Do what thou will philosophy". Some claim "Sgt Peppers" is dedicated to Crowley not only because he's on the cover, but it was released twenty years after his death in 1947, and it begins, "It was Twenty years ago today". *[Just as I got to this bit by the way, my computer cut out for no apparent reason, PC].* So leaving well alone. I'll let you make your own minds up, suffice to say that one of the above mentioned sites also claimed that top Christian band DC Talk were also of the dark side!

Remember You

Frank Ifield was born in Coventry November 30th 1937, and became the first artist in UK history to achieve a hat trick of number ones in one year. Such was his stardom on December 2nd 1962 the Beatles supported Frank at and died a death in front of a partisan crowd. The tables soon turned of course and The Beatles went on to dominate world music. Bizarrely, a very collectable US album featuring both Frank and the Beatles was released by Vee-Jay Records in 1964.

've' Just Seen A Face

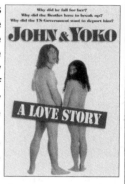

've' just seen a face and it was John and Yoko, well not this ime. It was in fact Mark McGann and Kim Myori, filming the 1985 film "John and Yoko-A Love Story". The film crew came o the city and re-enacted the Acorn ceremony. The 2 minute egment begins with a white Rolls Royce pulling up in Priory St outside the cathedral steps. There appears to be a bench of orts in the trailer attached to the car, but we never actually ee it (I suspect it was a cardboard prop). The couple leave he car along with Anthony Fawcett with the plastic cups in and. As they walk up towards the Cathedral ruins, they are reeted by hoardes of press and fans. John is asked where is wife is, he doesn't reply. He is then asked if he has come o see the exhibition, he retorts to laughter, "I think we are the xhibition". The scene changes to what is supposed to be the Deanery, it's actully The Navy Room inside the Cathedral. This is where Yoko and The Canon egan arguing that age old question what is art? Clearly Canon Verney felt that lanting acorns under a metal seat was not art. The last segment is John planting ne acorns, with the old cathedral spire in the background. The actors were ressed pretty much as their real-life counter-parts on the day (John & Yoko specially). All in all they put in a pretty good show, and its good to see very little oetic licence in evidence.

Left, The Navy Room circa 2006. Right John & Yoko plant their film Acorns.

Still and cover courtesy of Sony Video.

Bev Jones

From Coventry, released a stream of first class singles in the 1960's. A true vocal powerhouse hence constant comparisons to Brenda Lee. Bev did a show with the Beatles, "Afterwards I went to the Beatles dressing room", said Bev, "to get their autographs (for my little cousin). John invited me in and I had a coffee with him. He asked me where I was from I replied Coventry, he laughed when I asked him the same question".

The Lennon Bench

There was another re-enactment of the Acorns story, (o rather The Bench) This was part of the City Stories dramas performed by professional Coventry theatre company "Theatre Absolute". The 15 minute play "The Lennor Bench" took place in Priory Gardens Coventry in June 2004. Written by Chris O'Connell and produced by Julia Negus it gives the story of John & Yoko's visit a comedic slant. A white bench was also made (built by Mike Royce by the way) for this production, looking very similar to the original one. Chris O'Connell "This was also the one used by Yoko when she returned in 2005. "It was a rapid-fire fast-moving story that took place shortly after John and Yoko's white bench, wa removed from the exhibition We concentrated on the anarchy and the charisma c John Lennon. That he was a misunderstood genius - why couldn't the world, wh couldn't Coventry understand that he had a vision? "

Brian Matthew

Brian was born on Sept 7th 1928 In Westwood Road Coventry. He later moved to Billing Road and was educated at Bablake School. He was probably one of the best-known DJ's of the early sixties, his voice was (and still is) like that of a kindly uncle. Despite his huge reputation as a DJ and Radio presenter he originally started out as an actor. He studied at RADA and had much experience in rep. His broadcasting career began in 1948 in Germany. He joined the BBC in 1954 and presented classic shows such as Saturday Club, Late Night Extra and Be My Guest. He also hosted the seminal TV show Thank Your Lucky Stars. Though Saturday Club (originally Saturday Skiffle Club in 1957) re mains his finest moment, with some 14 appearances by the Beatles.

They first appeared in January 1963, and pretty much made it their own. It became a perfect platform for their dry 'scouse' humour, especially at Christmas time, then the audience was treated to seasonal messages and the like. Brian even appeared on their Live at the BBC album, and his Beatle interviews have turned up on many bootleg LP's. In 1988 Brian was named Music Media personality of the Year. He still broadcasts on BBC Radio 2 on Saturday mornings on Sound of the Sixties.

The Orchids

Georgina Johnstone, Née Oliver was a third of Britain's first real girl group The Orchids. Although this Coventry trio of fifteen-year-old schoolgirls never quite made the charts, they created quite a buzz in the music world of the sixties. This is Georgina's story. She's the one in the glasses by the way.

We were present at the special edition Juke Box Jury that was held at a theatre in Liverpool with the Beatles as the jury. It was at the Empire Theatre on Dec. 7th. 1963. As a youngster the theatre seemed to me to be very big. We were seated waaaay up in the upper balcony. They played "Love Hit Me". Only Paul voted it a "hit". I don't think we were really bothered about whether they they voted it a hit or a miss. We were just so excited at the prospect of actually meeting them. Sorry to say that never happened. After the vote David Jacobs did the bit about "Well boys, it just so happens that we have the girls in the audience" and the audience let out a big 'Aaaahhh!' when we stood up and took the applause. I do have a memory of one of them (don't know which) shouting "Sorry, girls!" and I remember John shouting, 'I'll buy a hundred". Then it was over no heart stopping backstage visit, no autographs, nothing! As you would say we felt completely gutted! I have no memory of traveling to Liverpool or returning home. The picture in my mind is of us high up in the theatre and the Beatles looking small and indistinguishable a long way down on the stage.

The only other connection, if you can call it that, is that in one article reporting our first release, "Gonna Make Him Mine", the headline calls us "Coventry's Answer to the Beatles". It goes on to say, "....a new recording team that has been compared with the sensational Liverpool group, the Beatles." It doesn't say who said it or whether we were compared favourably or otherwise!

Steve and Heather Taylor

Local songwriters from Coventry, have clocked up seven entries in the Guinness book of Hit Singles. For artists like Daniel O'Donnell, Shaking Stevens and The Coventry City FA Cup Squad. On 9th September 1987 at the Dolphin Brassiere, Dolphin Square, London they had a close encounter of the 'Macca' kind. It was part of the Buddy Holly song contest that formed part of The Buddy Holly week celebrations. The ten songwriting winners were invited to dine with Paul and Linda and various other celebrities. Jonathan Ross presented the certificate awards to the ten winners. "We entered a song called "Love Attack", reveals Steve, "which has since been a hit for Shaky (Stevens). We were busy still sorting out "Go For It!" when we heard about the competition, there were only two days to go till the closing date and the song had to be written, recorded and posted; hopefully to arrive in time. We sent it off then promptly, forgot all about it and then 6 weeks later two invites arrived in the post, saying Paul and Linda invite you to rave on at the Dolphin. We couldn't believe it". "Linda was lovely to us" Heather said, "and came over to our table and asked which song we had written, we said "Love Attack" she said "Oh I love that one, I have the songs on a tape and I play them in the kitchen". We had a chat with Paul at his table and asked whether he'd seen the F.A.Cup final and Coventry beating Spurs. we said we'd written the Cup Final song and he said "That's Great" Steve said that we only had a morning to do the song because we'd only found out at short notice about the competition and Paul said "That's sheer luxury". "We only had a day to do a whole album!" He signed a certificate and I said it would have been nice if you'd signed the certificate in the frame and he retorted "what do you want for nutthin". At one point in the conversation we both turned round and thought my god he's speaking to us! We were both walking on air for about six weeks after".

Heather (standing) with Duane Eddy and Paul and Linda McCartney.

Steve Rouse

Steve Rouse is one of Coventry's top Beatles fanatics. Steve has a house full of Beatles collectable vinyl, books, displays and photos. "The year is 1976 and I'm still at school", Steve relates, "I didn't like school very much, except art. Not because I could paint, but because my Art teacher Mr Tool had a copy of Help.

that's where it all started for me. It still sounds just as great, and I still get shivers down the old spine listening to Revolver. I've been really lucky and met 3 out of 4 of The Beatles (God I wish John had stayed in England). Yes I'm a huge fan of The Four Lads From Liverpool, Who Shook the World, and Coventry Too!"

There's A Place

And the place is Coventry; and the question is, does Macca have a 'thing' about this city? I only ask because it seems to be a place that comes easily to his mind, and to prove I'm not getting a little carried away I can give at least four examples of Paul namedropping Coventry. Maybe it's because he picked up a speeding ticket here (see over), that he can't forget the place!

Let It Be As previously mentioned back on page 10, Mr. McCartney (as he was in those days) is seen in the "Let It Be" motion picture discussing with a very 'laid back' Lennon the pros and cons of live performance. He talks about the Matrix date in *Coventry,* and remembers that it was the worse first night nerves they ever had. Maybe Coventry sticks in his mind for that reason alone, who knows?

Thrillington Of course the ultra collectable orchestral version of Paul and Linda's classic second album Ram. It was called *Thrillington* under the name of Percy Thrills' Thrillington and released in 1971. On the rear of the sleeve the fictitious biography begins Percy "Thrills" Thrillington was born in *Coventry Cathedral* in 1939! Why Coventry Cathedral? Was there some connection with John's 1968 visit?

Anthology Look on page 86 in the Beatles Anthology book, and Paul is talking about double-booked gigs. Saying. "Birmingham was a hard gig, they would double book us with places close together, (so) *they* thought (like) Wolverhampton and Birmingham and Wolverhampton and *Coventry*". The odd thing is I can see no evidence of this ever happening as far as Coventry is concerned. Though I believe the night they played Nuneaton Co-op Hall they also had another engagement in Birmingham (see page 10), maybe Paul got the two Midland towns confused?

Liverpool Oratorio Movement II of this classical work by Sir Paul McCartney, depicting Liverpool schoolboys extolling the virtues of being born in Liverpool. The piece of course lists many other towns where the boys 'were not' born. So wouldn't you just know there's one Midlands city guaranteed to be mentioned, you've guessed it *Coventry.* Indeed Coventry is not only included but it also gets it's own separate line (in a nice bass voice). Unlike Birmingham, Edinburgh, Manchester and Sunderland who are rather lumped together. Other places mentioned include Solihull and Scarborough.

Paul McCartney speeding case again adjourned

The case against Beatle Paul McCartney, accused of exceeding the 40 m.p.h. speed limit along Fletchamstead Highway, Coventry, was adjourned a further 14 days by Coventry Magistrates today.

The magistrates were told that no Road Fund licence had yet been received from McCartney in response to a first notice asking for it.

A second notice would now be sent out.

McCartney is also accused of driving without a Road Fund licence.

On the 20th of July 1968, Jane Asher announced on the Simon Dee show, that her engagement to Paul McCartney was off! Apparently she had come home unexpectedly and found Macca 'entertaining' another lady! Paul was not happy and attempted to sack Jane's brother Peter from the fledgling Apple organisation. Paul's whereabouts for a couple of days were unknown. We do know however that on 22nd July he was caught speeding on the Fletchhamstead Highway in Coventry. It would seem Paul was just passing through the city, but where had he been or where was he going? Could he have been on his way back to London after telling his folks in Liverpool his side of the Jane Asher split story? It's all conjecture on my part, but clearly Mr McCartney was not a happy bunny.

So here are the events of that summers day in Coventry, Paul was heading down the Fletchhamstead Highway in his Aston Martin DB6. When he got between the Canley traffic island by the Fletchamstead police and fire brigade stations and the Fletchamstead traffic lights on the junction of Tile Hill Lane and the Standard cinema, he was nicked. (The building that was the Standard Cinema can be seen extreme right in the top photo on page 38, just behind the Matrix). When stopped and told of the offence, Paul said, "I am far too busy to bother about this". He gave his address as 95 Wigmore St, London (the original Apple HQ), and went on to say to the officer, "It's A fair cop, I thought I was doing just over 40". He was actually doing something between 55 and 60 mph according to Chief Inspector Arthur Osman. Not only was he speeding but his tax disc was four months out of date!

In a letter to the court The Beatle said, "I admit keeping an unlicensed vehicle. It was an oversight on the part of the people who look after my affairs. But of course I realise I am personally and ultimately responsible". His case though was adjourned four times. A spokesman for Apple declared, "The licence has gone off by registered post. There has been a lot of confusion and it has been difficult to find the licence". Apparently the three summonses had got mixed up with fan mail. He was eventually fined £15, and got his licence endorsed and was ordered to pay £8 6s 8d back duty, Paul did not appear in court. How strange that this should happen right by The Matrix, where the Beatles played in 1962, bearing in mind this area is a few miles out of the City Centre! Interesting that Paul came to the city just 37 days after John & Yoko's visit. Making Paul (as far as we know) the last Beatle to visit the city!

We assume the following songs were not played at the trial...Lovely Rita, Day Tripper, Drive My Car, Ticket To Ride, Back Seat Of My Car, Why Don't We Do It In The Road, I Should Have Known Better, The Long and Winding Road, Taxman, Not Guilty, Slow Down, Band On The Run and You Know My Name (Look Up The Number). **With many thanks to Kalman Roskone & The Coventry Telegraph.**

Think For Yourself

This one has been doing my nut in for the last few months. The Vampires were one of Coventry's first Rock 'n' Roll bands and were fronted by local kingpin Vince Martin. Vince is a great friend of mine and he maintains that they once had the Beatles support them at the Nuneaton Co-op Hall in 1961 (there was even a two-page spread in the local paper about it!) Memories are fading fast but Vince remembers that it was a Wednesday night, Reg Calvert was the promoter and Pete Best was probably still with them (in 1961 he would have been). He also

has a vague recollection that they played in leather (as does the Vampires guitarist Jon Buggins). A year or so later Vince remembers travelling to a gig and the Beatles coming on the radio, he recalls saying something like, "that's that band that supported us in Nuneaton"! Yet there is no evidence in any of the books that this gig ever happened. Having said that, no books until this now have ever revealed that the October 5th gig in Nuneaton happened. If it did happen it would be a remarkable story and would be the first time that the Fab Four had played in the Midlands. Vince said he once had the poster for the gig. If only such evidence had survived.

Hannah Tobin a Coventry Beatles Fan

"As I write this I am watching the Beatles Anthology Series on DVD and John Lennon has just said, regarding the break-up of the group, "You have all the old records there if you wanna reminisce". Well for me, it's not a case of reminiscing. I think it was 1995 that I first really noticed The Beatles. I was 13 and they were a band who had split up 25 years earlier, but there was just something about them that caught my eye - Or ears! My Dad owned the 'Red' and 'Blue' albums and the Anthology 1 album on vinyl Gradually, I started to play them more than him and by the time Anthology 2 was released, I was hooked! I had got The Beatle bug! In 1997 I attended my first Beatles Week Festival in Liverpool and met John Lennon's sister, Julia Baird, Bob Wooler - The Cavern DJ and John Lennon's Uncle Charlie!"

"It was a fab first festival as I watched many tribute bands (Some from Brazil and Japan) in Mathew Street and ate strawberries and cream in the grounds of Strawberry Field on a beautiful sunny afternoon. A couple of years later, I had a chance to visit and record in the world famous Abbey Road Studios. I had entered a nationwide competition by singing 'With A Little Help From My Friends' down the telephone. I then got through to the regional finals and sang, 'Come Together'. It was a dream come true when I actually won and with the 99 other winners went to London and re-recorded, 'Karma Chameleon' with Boy George for charity. Studio 2, where most of The Beatles' songs were recorded definitely has a magical vibe to it! Everyone in my 6th Form class (Including the teachers!) wanted to know about my trip. People asked me about Boy George, but the highlight for me was just being there in Abbey Road Studios!

Other Beatle experiences include Paul McCartney's concert in Birmingham in 2003 and the Concert For George in November 2002. I don't think anything will ever top that night. Seeing all of George Harrison's friends on stage, playing his music and all of us there to remember him – A wonderful show for one of my favourite Beatles. Yoko Ono's trip to Coventry in October 2005 will be an afternoon I shall remember forever! It started off a normal day until I checked my e-mails at lunchtime. In one message a friend casually asked, "Are you going to see Yoko at the Cathedral today?" I had no idea she was coming, but it had been announced on the local radio Breakfast show. I quickly grabbed my camera and dashed to the Cathedral - Not knowing whether I had already missed her! When I arrived I could see camera crews and reporters gathering around 'Unity Lawn'. I asked someone what was happening and they gave me the good news that the tree planting ceremony was due to begin in an hour! I felt so lucky to witness this piece of history in the making and as I had got there early I had a brilliant view! After the ceremony Yoko gave interviews and signed many autographs, but I was too nervous to go up and say hello - Even though I was standing next to her at one point! But it was a beautiful afternoon and whenever I walk past the trees I always think of that day in October and of course, John and Yoko. I only wish I could've been around to see their first visit to Coventry in 1968 - Along with The Beatles' concerts at The Matrix and The Coventry Theatre. Can anyone build me a time machine?" Check her great website out at www.hanmade.co.uk

Tony Cooper

Having mentioned two of Coventry's Top Beatles fans, Hannah and Steve Rouse I think it only right we also mention Tony Cooper from Nuneaton, who has also spent a life collecting rare Beatles albums. Having worked in Russia he was able to get his hands on some rare Soviet issues. The highlight of his collection however is the now famous Yesterday and Today album, the infamous "Butchers Sleeve".

Tomorrow Never Knows

.....If you're going to be famous or not. One Coventry band who have a wealth of talent are The Circle. A now band with a soul that grew up in the 60's. The Beatles figure heavily as far as influences, especially for Jim Peakman. This is what he thought about playing at the Cavern. "As soon as I found out we had a gig at The Cavern I was excited. Been a Beatle fan all my life, I always wanted to play there. When first parking up in Liverpool there was an instant buzz going around. Everyone was on a high. I can remember thinking whilst I was carrying my guitar and amp down the stairs wow Jim you've made it this far, how cool, is this? I've achieved a life time goal To my surprise there was a 60s Mersey beat days going on in the old part of the venue. This meant the old bands from back in the Beatles days were playing there. Well that was it for me; I stayed in the old side until I was onstage listening to these old rockers singing classics like What I Say (Ray Charles), Dizzy Miss Lizzy and Money. Later in the evening I got talking to some of these bands. (One of which was out in Hamburg with the Beatles). I left with memories of a great day out. Check them out at www.thecircleonline.com

Tony Beard

Tony was once a member of Bob Tempest and The Buccaneers and is a great fund raiser in Coventry, especially for the Coventry Myton Hospice who looked after his late wife Helen. Tony's generosity has helped fund this book so here's a special advert for Tony's favourite Charity...

The Coventry Myton Hospice Appeal is a campaign to raise £5M to build and equip a new hospice in Coventry. A shortfall of between 20-25 hospice beds in the Coventry and Warwickshire area has existed for many years.

During 2005, the Appeal reached the half-way mark towards its target of £5M and by Autumn of 2005 the Appeal had passed £3M. Consequently, the dream of a new hospice in Coventry is now moving closer to becoming a reality, thanks to the hard work, enthusiasm and support of a large group of committed supporters of the hospice.

Myton Hamlet Hospice, Myton Road, Warwick, CV34 6PX
Telephone 01926 838818 or 02476 411177
Fax 01926 409110 Email coventry.appeal@mytonhospice.org

Top, the Harrison Cheque, Middle left Rob Armstrong and the finished "Harrison" guitar. Middle right, Joe Brown Hillary Giltrap (Gordon's wife) and Rob. Bottom left the initialled tailpiece from model #464.

Try Some, Buy Some

Non-Coventry folk may not be familiar with the name Rob Armstrong. Rob Is one of Coventry's most enduring musical characters, a musician in his own right but a guitar maker by trade. Rob's superb custom-built stringed instruments have been used by the likes of Gordon Giltrap Alvin Lee, Joe Brown, Bert Jansch, Martin Barre and George Harrison.

Yes George was the proud owner of a Armstrong Baby Acoustic Guitar'. I asked Rob how he came to make a instrument for George. "Well my association with George Harrison began when I got a call from my good friend Gordon Giltrap telling me that he had met Joe Brown, who happens to be one of my heroes. Joe apparently was very impressed with my guitars, and wanted to meet me and buy one. Of course this sounded great to me, many of us still have those first LP's we ever buy and one of mine was Joe's Browns, he was a remarkable talent. So we went to Joe's house and Alvin Lee turned up, he bought one as well. Then Joe Brown asked me to make one of the small guitars, or Baby Guitar, so he could give it to George as a present that was 1992". George's guitar was number #464 and has his initials G.H. on the tailstock.

"Then five years later In 1997 I got a phone call from George and he asked me to make two similar guitars to the one I had made for him. One of them was a present for his son Dhani and the other one was a present for Paul Stewart son of former racing driver Jackie Stewart. So that's what I did, the numbers for those were #596 and #597". I asked about the conversation he had with George, " It was a business call really, with George just discussing his requirements". So did he have to wait a while for it to be made like everyone else I asked? "I'm afraid he did, no preferential treatment even for a former Beatle". "I was always a Beatle fan", Rob admits, "Isn't everyone? The thing about George from a guitarist's point of view, is the way he tuned his guitars, he just tuned it to the song he was playing at the time. Anyone picking that instrument up afterwards would find it to be out of tune. Most people tune their guitars to a tuner; George had this ability as a guitarist just to tune it by ear. That's how he achieved his distinctive style, because some of the notes are a little bit flat and some are a bit sharp and some a bit wobbly, he was a very free guitar player. I think it comes with using the ukulele a lot as George did, it's very open tuning the "My Dogs Has Fleas" method really. Sometimes an instrument sounds better when it's tuned a little bit sharp or flat"

"The interesting thing about that guitar, Rob continues," it's probably the most expensive guitar I have ever made. If ever it came up in auction it would probably make a small fortune.". On that subject Rob has also never cashed the Harrison cheque, preferring to keep it framed along with the plectrum George sent him. "I have no intention of selling it, but a George Harrison cheque is probably worth more than £1.840.00 he paid for the two guitars".

Turned Out Nice Again

The connection here is of Alan Randall, the world's greatest George Formby impersonator, being featured on a Beatles video. He was born near Coventry in the town of Bedworth, Warwickshire. More about him later, but as we are discussing The Beatles, ukulele's and George Formby I figure we may as well have the whole story. So in case there is anyone out there from another planet, a ukulele (meaning "Dancing Flea" in Hawaiian) is a small four stringed guitar that originated in Hawaii, we also have the ukulele-banjo, a small four stringed banjo favoured by Formby. The Beatles drew their influences from many quarters; some obvious ones like Chuck Berry and Elvis Presley, others less obvious ones like George Formby.

Singer and Actor George Formby was famed in the 1940's and 50's for his risqué double-entendre songs like "My Little Stick of Blackpool Rock" and "When I'm Cleaning Windows". He, like most music hall based comedians, knew never to cross the line, and George had the perfect look to deliver such songs. Without causing offence he could never be accused of being handsome, but his gaunt looks and protruding teeth fitted in perfectly with his coy persona. With ukulele-banjo in hand and twinkle in his eye, George was a huge star, and his most famous song "Leaning On A Lamppost" is still well known to all ages today. His catch phrase, "Turned Out Nice Again", is still often used by us Brit's especially when a rainy day finishes on a sunny note (usually delivered in a Formby-style Lancashire accent).

George at the Gorge Formby convention. *Picture courtesy of Dennis Taylor & The George Formby Society*

The Beatles were all well aware of Formby when growing up in Liverpool and his influence on them would make an appearance from time to time. He seemed a perfect choice to have been on the iconic Sgt: Peppers cover collage but he never was, though his influence at least is contained within that LP on the song "When I'm Sixty Four". It's interesting that time travelling TV Sitcom "Goodnight Sweetheart" did an episode that saw George Formby singing this very song (an actor of course).

John Lennon's mum Julia was an accomplished Ukulele player (as was her Father) she in turn showed John how to play the instrument. So little wonder why some of John's 'one-offs have a Formby edge to them, especially his "Isadora Duncan worked for Telefunken" ditty from the "Let It Be" feature film.

Paul McCartney has had his Formby moments too, as well as producing the single "I'm The Urban Spaceman" for The Bonzo Dog Band; he also played ukulele-banjo on the track. Then we have the George Harrison classic "Something". Paul would play the song on the ukulele as a tribute to George on his 2003 Back In The World Tour. Always informing the audience that George was a great Ukulele player and a huge George Formby fan. Macca would often speed the song up and add the odd Formby impression just for good measure. In Anthology Paul says, "To this day, if I ever meet grownups who play the ukulele I love em!"

Then there was George Harrison, the biggest Ukulele and George Formby fan of all the Beatles. He not only loved playing the instrument but had a large collection (it was claimed he had one in each room of his home) and was a member of the George Formby Society. Not just a member by name, Mr. Harrison actually attended a society convention in Blackpool with his family and actor/singer Jimmy Nail. He apparently was happy to sign autographs for everyone and even got up and sang and played along to 'In My Little Snapshot Album'. His son Dhani also played the ukulele at the event. In the Beatles Anthology George is seen chatting with Paul and Ringo at Friar Park about their time in India and plays on the ukulele a unreleased song he wrote at the time entitled "Dera Dhun" (often spelt Derradune on bootlegs, he also plays a uke' version of "Ain't She Sweet" but this was not included in the broadcast). In the foreground we also see a Resonator ukulele, just part of his large collection, a collection that also included Formby's rare "Ludwig" ukulele-banjo.

George was a true ukulele "nut" and recalls the story of how he and John Lennon were in the Greek Islands singing the Hare Krishna mantra with uke' accompaniment for hours and hours because they couldn't stop. Even Coventry kid Pete Waterman tells of George's great ukulele playing and their mutual love of George Formby. Paul McCartney also remembers how he and George would play their Ukulele's together at his home shortly before his death. It's interesting that George would also have a house in the land of the uke'; Hawaii. Getting back to Alan Randall, well Alan was born in 1934 in Bedworth, Warwickshire and became well known as being the world's number One George Formby impersonator (although he was a brilliant multi-instrumentalist and jazz musician to boot). Actually going on to co-write a musical based on the Ukulele-banjo king's life entitled "Turned Out Nice Again". He had played in Las Vegas and appeared with the likes of The Rolling Stones and Cliff Richard. He died of motor neurone disease in 2005. When the 'Threetles' put out their first come-back single "Free As A Bird" (of course a new recording bolted onto an old John Lennon demo), the video that accompanied it was a tour de force. Guaranteed to get every Beatle fan fired up looking for "hidden" (or in some cases "not so hidden") song titles. All great fun, but right at the end of the promo we see a ukulele playing figure on stage at a Victorian theatre taking a bow. This is none other than Alan Randall impersonating George Formby, along with the visuals we get a few seconds of ukulele-banjo

Left Alan Randall, and above the actual ukulele as featured on Free As A Bird.
Photos courtesy of Paul Woodhead who now owns the instrument.

and a backwards voice that sounds like it's saying "Made By John Lennon". When played backwards the message says, "Turned Out Nice Again, Didn't It", spoken apparently by John himself. Paul claims it was put on especially for all the "backward groove freaks", then claimed to be amazed when they heard it backwards and it sounded like it was saying "John Lennon", Paul took that as a thumbs-up from John for the project. Listening to the phrase both ways round, it's pretty obvious that it's all nicely contrived to sound like it does, the pronunciation of some of the words are dodgy to say the least. That won't stop the "Paul is Dead Brigade" of course!

George Harrison played the ukulele on "Free As A Bird" and apparently wanted to appear in the video, but Director John Pytka felt if George appeared in it then so should Ringo and Paul, so Alan Randall got the gig. The video quite rightly won a Grammy in 1997 and an Award for The Best Short form Music Video.

With A Little Help From My Friends

John Hague was a fellow art student with John Lennon back in Liverpool. When Mr. Hague needed a house in 1967 John Lennon stepped in and paid out £1,200 for a house in Leamington Spa, Warwickshire. It was very run down when purchased, but after lots of TLC it eventually won an architectural award. "We were good friends" Said Mr. Hague, "He would have given me anything in those days, I needed a place to live and he gave me this. John and Paul both sponsored an art exhibition for John H. Apparently this house was the place to be in the 60's. He had the best music and his art was all over the walls. He once ran an antiques shop in Leamington, but it has since changed hands and become a guitar shop, though John H still owns the property.

Miscellany *OK here's a random list of other Coventry/Beatles connections.*

When former Smiths guitarist Johnny Marr played the live music venue in Coventry The Colosseum in May 2000 his drummer was none other than Zak Starkey.

BBC Coventry & Warwickshire's football commentator Clive Eakin apparently went to the same primary school as Paul McCartney's kids. While former chief Executive of Warwickshire County Council Ian Caulfield was a classmate of Paul McCartney's at the Liverpool Institute. George Harrison also attended the school.

Coventry born Delia Derbyshire was a huge figure in the world of electronic music and her work for the BBC's Radiophonic Workshop was a big influence on the likes of John & Yoko, Paul McCartney and George Martin. Although she will be best remembered for arranging the original Doctor Who theme.

All four Beatles passed through Coventry recently, travelling first class from Euston to Lime Street on Virgin Trains. Sadly they were only their waxwork effigies being transported from Madame Tussauds to "The Beatles Story" in Liverpool.

Local musician Jim Kemp was an extra on the film John & Yoko A Love Story, he was also half of the CBS signed duo Jimmy, Jimmy who released a cover of All You Need Is Love. Whilst they were busking outside the Wogan Show (14-12-90) Macca sent a signed script out to them saying he liked what he had heard.

The now defunct Coventry Express published two colour Beatles specials. One in October 63 as a trailer to their November appearance in the City and another in 1964 covering their American success. Both papers are now highly collectable.

Former Coventry Evening Telegraph reporter Gerry Hunt talked to John Lennon in Bermuda in 1980, the year of his death. This information was part of a piece from Coventry Telegraph writer Dayle Crutchlow who did a feature on the Beatles in Coventry in 2000.

In 1984 Yoko Ono gave a donation of a £1.000 to Coventry's Rape Crisis Centre.

A former Coventry student Robin Maryon (and Beatle fan) was responsible for coming up with the logo for the Liverpool John Lennon Airport. The logo was of course based on a John Lennon self-portrait.

Coventry crooner Vince Hill has covered the songs "Here, There And Everwhere" and "Imagine".

In the early 60's John Lennon's Dad Freddy, worked at the Chesford Grange Hotel near Kenilworth, Warwickshire.

Coventry's Paul King of "King" fame sang on the number one charity single "Let It Be" as one of the many members of "Ferry Aid" (including Macca of course). The record was produced by Coventry's Pete Waterman in aid of the Sun's Zeebrugge Disaster Fund. Waterman along with Stock Aitken (of course), was also responsible for the number One "Ferry Across The Mersey" single that included Paul McCartney, The Christians, Gerry and the Pacemakers, and Holly Johnson

Peter and Gordon were part of the early Beatle inner sanctum. They also sang the song Lady Godiva and caused a stir by turning Coventry's most famous lady into a common stripper. The Lord Mayor of the time was not amused.

Terry Hall (not the Specials front-man) is a ventriloquist who had the lovable lion named Lenny or Lenny the Lion to give him his correct name. Although born in Oldham he did however marry a Coventry girl Dee Francis and they settled in the city (Terry Hall of course not Lenny *he's a puppet*). Lenny & Terry had a TV show called *Pops and Lenny* on May 16th 1963 the show featured The Beatles playing "Please, Please Me", "From Me To You" and joined in with the shows theme "After You've Gone"

The December 1962/January 1963 issue of the now famous Mersey Beat magazine includes a full page listing of the successes of that year entitled "1962 The Beatles year of achievement". Twelve locations are mentioned in the list of appearances including Coventry (Birmingham is also listed).

Top Coventry musician Bob Jackson was once a member of Badfinger, He recorded the "Head First" album with them at Apple studios. It was engineered by Phil MacDonald. He even got to meet Derek Taylor, he now plays in the Fortunes. His daughter Emily studied at The Liverpool Institute of Performing Arts and got to meet one of it's patrons Sir Paul McCartney during her degree ceremony.

"Are you In Coventry" is the name of a 'track' on the bootleg CD "Alf Together Now". The four-second track is of a woman saying "Are you in Coventry" then the click of a tape recorder. The album was a collection of rare Beatles tapes (recorded on their own portable tape machines) originally owned by former Beatles chauffer Alf Bicknell.

Beatle related exhibitions in the area have included Signed Yoko Ono prints at XU Limited Gallery, Leamington Spa. An exhibition of artwork by former Beatles LP Revolver cover artist Klaus Voormann was held at The Leamington Pump Rooms. Klaus was also a bass player in Manfred Mann and when Paul left the Beatles the initial idea was that Klaus would join John, George and Ringo in a band called the Ladders. Also, Cynthia Lennon made a guest appearance at the Owen Owen department store in 1986 (now Primark) to promote her fabric designs. Sgt Pepper cover-man Peter Blake held his Alphabet exhibition at Nuneaton Museum in 2005.

First up a huge amount of thanks go to my wife Julie for all her time and effort with this and all my other projects.

With Thanks To: The Beatles and all their fans, Roger Vaughan at Coventry City Council, Pete Walters at CV One, June Fairbrother at the Coventry Evening Telegraph, Mel at Mirrorpix, Rob Armstrong, Tony Beard, Anthony Fawcett, Apple, EMI, Hannah Tobin, Steve Rouse, Tony Campbell, Biffo Beech, Helen Shapiro, Coventry Cathedral, BBC Coventry & Warwickshire, Tony Cooper, Woodster Productions, Tony 'Banger' Walsh, Dayle Crutchlow, Diana Bellamy, Don Fardon, Post and Fastprint services, Local Studies at Coventry Central Library, Keith McMillan, Pete Waterman, Dennis Taylor & The George Formby Society, Brooklands Grange Hotel, Susan Moore, Bev Jones, Georgina Johnstone, The Fletch, HSS Tool Hire, Steve & Heather Taylor, John Harris, www.tamworthbands.com, Sony Pictures, Kalman Roskone, Paul Woodhead, Theatre Absolute and www.beatlesdays.com.

And special thanks and peace to Yoko Ono

For more information go to www.covmusic.net

STAY FAB

The photographs in this book have been collected from various sources and are used with the credit to the owners. While every effort has been made to trace all ownership there may be some incidents that this is not the case, we make no claim on the copyright on any such material. This is a self-produced labour of love project that I hope further highlights Coventry's place in world music. This book is totally unofficial (like I had to tell you that) and is not endorsed by Apple or Yoko Ono.

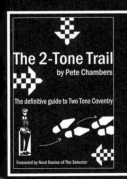

STILL AVAILABLE BY THIS AUTHOR

The 2-Tone Trail

The definitive guide to the real roots of Coventry's ska phenomenon.

Get it from E-bay just £5.00
plus postage
Or e-mail   tencton@hotmail.com   for more details.

Some recommended Beatles links.
(With thanks to Hannah Tobin)

- www.thebeatles.com ~ Official Website
- www.paulmccartney.com ~ Official Website
- www.georgeharrison.com ~ Official Website
- www.ringostarr.com ~ Official Website
- www.mplcommunications.com ~ Official Website
- www.cavern-liverpool.co.uk ~ This is the Cavern website!
- www.liveapool.com ~ A perfect site for anyone who wants to visit or find out more about The Beatles Liverpool.
- http://hollywoodandvine.com ~ This website is part of Capital Records
- http://thebeatleshop.co.uk/ ~ This is the official website for the FAB Beatles shop in Liverpool's Mathew Street.
- www.beatlesstory.co.uk ~ Visit the new Beatles Story museum website!
- www.petebest.com ~ Pete Best's Official Website!
- www.ringotour.com ~ This is Ringo Starr's official tour page!
- www.instantkarma.com ~ One of the best John Lennon/Yoko Ono and Julian and Sean Lennon websites!
- www.stuck-inside-a-cloud.net ~ One of the best George Harrison fan sites on the net!
- http://www.liverpoolbeatlescene.com ~ This site provides Beatles news from the Beatle City of Liverpool.
- http://www.fabfour.addr.com ~ This is The Beatles London News and Information Service website.
- http://www.beatlesusa.com ~ This is a fab USA based Beatles fan site!
- http://www.beatleworld.co.uk ~ An amazing Beatles website!
- http://www.tributesabroad.co.uk/tune/info_beatles_fab4.html ~ Website of the Beatles tribute band The Fab 4
- http://www.a-i-u.net/ ~ Approximately Infinite Universe, a great Yoko website
- http://www.fabfour.addr.com/oldsite/links.htm ~Steve Clifford's great webpage
- http://www.eskimo.com/~bpentium/beatles.html ~The Beatles At The Web Spot, loads of info
- http://www.beatles-discography.com/ ~The Beatles Discography Com, a truly inspired site
- http://www.beatles-unlimited.com/ ~ The e-home of the Beatles Unlimited Magazine
- http://www.beatlefans.com/ ~ Home of Beatle Fans Com, a marvellously informed site
- http://rocksgodiva.tripod.com/thebeatlessenttocoventry/~ This is my Beatles Sent To Coventry Site

CABIN STUDIOS LIMITED

82 London Road, Coventry CV1 2JT
Tel.No. 02476 220749
www.cabinstudio.co.uk

24-track digital and analogue recording classic microphones and outboard gear studio area and control room acoustically designed friendly and professional staff

Past clients include- The La`s-The Primitives McAlmont-Catatonia-Tony Iomi-Steve Swindells Sonic Boom-Pauline Black-Terry Hall -Buster Bloodvessel-JonMoss-Diesel Park West -Graham Fellows etc.,

VINTAGE TACKLE

Offering customers reasonably priced, modern new fishing tackle also good quality used items. There is also a large selection of ground bait and frozen bait available. We also buy used tackle or part exchange on new items.

For further information contact Ron on 07816936352 or e-mail ron.farmer@ntlworld.com

COVENTRY MARKET
STALL 95

In addition we cater for the traditional angler with a range of vintage reels, rods and traditional hand made floats. A small deposit will secure items for one month. Fishing related items always wanted, e.g. books, china etc.

THE DOG & TRUMPET

HERTFORD STREET COVENTRY

Long-established alternative Friday venue. Goth, industrial, punk, 80s, indie, plus live bands and open until late

Coming soon
Motown Night

Fantastic for lunches from 11.45am - 2.30pm.
£2.85 per meal, two meals £5.00.

Coventry's own "Cavern"

DON'T FORGET TO CHECK OUT OUR SPECIALS ON MEALS

Coventry City Mad
Unofficial Sky Blues

www.coventrycity-mad.co.uk

Coventry City Mad
Unofficial Sky Blues

www.coventrycity-mad.co.uk

Coventry City Mad
Unofficial Sky Blues

Woodster Management

Woodster Management

Artist Management and Rehearsal Studio

www.woodster-productions.com

www.myspace.com/woodster1

mark@woodster-productions.com

Presents

TONY "BANGER" WALSH

Brilliant After Dinner Speaker, Actor

STILL MINDING HIS OWN BUSINESS!!

An after dinner speaker you will not forget. Drawing on his many years as a former ITV "World of Sport" wrestling star and his subsequent career in the world of close protection, Tony is a guaranteed crowd puller!

PERSONALITY ARTISTES LTD

Worldwide Headquarters
PO Box 1 Blackpool
FY6 7WS United Kingdom
E-Mail: info@personalityartistes.com
www.personalityartistes.com

Contact Mal Ford
or Jean Parkes
Tel: +44(0)1253 899988
Fax: +44(0)1253 882823
www.malford.com

COVSUPPORT NEWS SERVICE

Serving The Needs Of The Sky Blue Generation

http://covsupport.homestead.com/index.html

ALL THE LATEST BEATLES NEWS! WITH REGULAR UPDATES!

DETAILS OF THE PREMIER BEATLES EVENT IN THE CAPITAL!

DETAILS OF EVENTS IN THE UK, USA & EUROPE!

LOADS OF BEATLES ITEMS FOR SALE!

JOIN OUR MAILING LIST AND GET EVENT DETAILS BY E-MAIL!
SEE PICTURES FROM PAST EVENTS IN OUR PHOTO GALLERY!

www.beatlesdays.com

The Albany Club

The best new live entertainment venue in Coventry

Sunday - Free & Easy/ Jam Session
Friday - Live bands
Saturday - Various live entertainment
Plus many one off events

To see top class artists and some of the best bands the UK has to offer check out the website at

www.albanyclub.co.uk

10 Earlsdon St. Earlsdon, Coventry. CV5 6EG Tel : 024 7667 5375

Herbert
Media

Audio. Video. New Media

The Herbert, Jordan Well
Coventry CV1 5QP

T: 024 7683 2310
F: 024 7683 4080
E: info@theherbert.org
W: www.theherbert.org

COVENTRY CATHEDRAL

Home to John Lennon & Yoko Ono's 1968 'Acorn Event'

Cathedral open daily
9.00am – 5.00pm admission FREE
See the 'John & Yoko' Japanese Oak Trees Dedicated by Yoko Ono in 2005

Call 024 7652 1200
Visit www.coventrycathedral.org.uk
Guided tours available (charges apply)
Also contact us for details of forthcoming events and exhibitions or conference bookings

Covered In Print

Books and magazines always wanted-cash paid

Second hand books - Book Search
Out of Print Copies
Large Assortment of Rare Volumes
Pre-Decimal Paperbacks
Comics-Maps - Ephemera
1st Editions - Children's Books
Sports and Hobbies - 8mm & 16mm Film

Coventry Market, Stall 56/96
Phone: 07890 819136

Here are some more adverts but these are from November 1963

"PLEASE, PLEASE ME"
SING THE BEATLES
PLEASE, PLEASE YOU?
CERTAINLY SIR!

WITH A COLLARLESS STYLED SUIT
AS WORN BY THE BEATLES

From

YOUNG IDEAS SHOP
372 FOLESHILL ROAD
(opp. Livingstone Road)

A Department of

LOCKHURST LANE CO-OP SOCIETY

Get Your Record-breaking Collarless Suit Now!

"PLEASE PLEASE ME"
sing the Beatles

YOU will certainly be pleased by the selection of BEATLE singles, L.P's and E.P's

at

L. STEVENSON
583 STONEY STANTON ROAD
(Opposite Broad Street)
Telephone Coventry 88224

HUNT THE BEATLES

Win
- An autographed photo of the Beatles
- Six Beatles sweaters with Beatles badges
- Membership of the famous Beatles Fan Club

See page 19

COMING NEXT WEEK
THE BEATLES

THIS IS THE COVER OF THEIR LATEST L.P.

★

THE BIGGEST STOCK IN THE MIDLANDS WILL BE AT

JILL HANSON'S
RECORD SHOP
8 MARKET WAY, COVENTRY

FOR YOUNG MEN
★ BEATLE JACKETS ★
From £3-15-0 and £5-2-6 in Cord, Barathea and Foam etc.

GIBBERDS
THE LOWER PRECINCT